Craft Fun!

NORTH LIGHT BOOKS

Cincinnati, Ohio

A Note About Safety

The activities in this book were developed for the enjoyment of children. We've taken every precaution to ensure their safety and success. Please follow the directions, and note where an adult's help is required. In fact, feel free to work alongside your young artists as often as you can. They will appreciate help in reading and learning new techniques, and will love the chance to talk and show off their creations. Children thrive on attention and praise, and craft adventures are the perfect setting for both.

Library of Congress Cataloging-in-Publication Data

Craft fun
    p.   cm.—(Art & activities for kids)
  Summary: Presents instructions for a variety of craft projects, including yarn baskets, clay puppets, beads, button designs, tie-dye t-shirts, puzzle cards, gifts, costumes, and more.
  ISBN 0-89134-834-4
  1. Handicraft—Juvenile literature. [1. Handicraft.] I. Series.
TT160.C698   1997
745.5—dc21   97-370
                                                        CIP
                                                        AC

Edited by Julie Wesling Whaley
Design Direction by Clare Finney
Art Direction by Kristi Kane Cullen
Photography by Pamela Monfort
Very special thanks to Theresa Brockman, Eric Deller, Jessica Dolle, Anita Drake, Libby Fellerhoff, Chris Keefe, Alison Wenstrup, Suzanne Whitaker and Rachel Wolf.

Table of Contents

(Table of Contents continued on page 4) ▶

Be a Good Artist

Work Habits

Get permission to set up a craft workshop before you begin. Cover your workspace with newspapers or a vinyl tablecloth. Wear a smock or big, old shirt to protect your clothes. Cut the long sleeves off of the shirt so you won't drag them through paint or glue.

Always get permission to use photographs or things that might be important. Always get permission before you decorate any clothes. Practice on scrap paper or old clothes before working on good clothes. Work slowly and carefully.

If you work on new clothes, wash and dry them before you begin. Put wax paper between layers of cloth so the paint or dye won't "bleed" through to the back. Some of the things you might use to make clothes fun, like permanent markers and dye, could be harmful, so *always get an adult to help you.*

If you are careless, you could hurt yourself while you're making crafts. Have fun, but be careful and treat all your tools with respect. Sweep up scraps and clean up splatters and spills as soon as they happen. Always finish by cleaning your workspace and all of your tools.

Craft Terms

Crafts. People create crafts when they make household things by hand. Craftspeople are very careful to make things sturdy as well as beautiful; this quality is known as "fine craftsmanship." There are many traditional crafts, with techniques and designs that have been handed down from crafter to crafter for many generations.

Glue. Most of the projects in this book can be done with regular white glue. For projects where you use cloth, **fabric glue** works better because it's specially made for cloth. Look for a label that says "permanent" or "washable." **Carpenter's glue** from a hardware store works best on heavy materials like wood.

Paint. You can use tempera paint, acrylic paint, or fabric paint to decorate your crafts. **Tempera paint**, or poster paint, works well on paper and cardboard. **Acrylic** is a thick, water-based paint that works well on wood, plastic, metal or clay. **Fabric paint** is best for cloth, because it won't wash out. There are many kinds of fabric paint, including glitter paint and puffy paint. You can also paint on clothes with **latex house paint**, because it doesn't wash out.

Most kinds of fabric paint are *nontoxic*, which means they are very safe. They will have "nontoxic" on their label. Other paints do not say "nontoxic," which means they could be harmful. *Always get permission* to use fabric paint before you begin. The same goes for dyes and permanent markers.

Follow the directions carefully for each project. When you see this symbol, have an adult help you.

The clock symbol means you must wait to let something dry before going on to the next step. It is very important not to rush ahead.

Don't put art materials in your mouth. If you're working with a younger child, don't let him put art materials in his mouth, either.

Watercolor paint. This is a water-based paint that is transparent—you can see through it when you paint with it. It comes in little trays of dry paint that you wet with a paintbrush and water. You'll need this for some projects in Part Four.

Paintbrushes. There are many kinds of brushes for different uses. You may want to buy several, from fine-point watercolor brushes to square, heavy-bristle brushes. It's fun to paint with big brushes from the hardware store, too!

Varnish. Acrylic gloss medium is a nontoxic varnish sold at art supply stores. Acrylic varnish is safest to use because it's nontoxic. Clear nail polish makes a good varnish, but get permission before you use it.

Ruler. Keep a ruler handy for measuring. This symbol, ", means inches—12" means 12 inches; cm mean centimeter. There are about 2½ centimeters in 1 inch. This symbol, ', means feet; m means meter. There are about 3 feet in 1 meter.

Masking tape is strong enough to hold cardboard or fabric. Wide masking tape holds better than thin masking tape. **Duct tape** is even stronger, but it is harder to use because it's so sticky. You can buy either kind of tape at a supermarket or hardware store.

Fabric is another word for cloth. For most of the projects in this book, natural fabric such as cotton will work better than synthetic fabric like polyester. Experiment on scraps before you work on good clothes.

A **garment** is something you wear, like a shirt, jacket, cap or shoes. You can decorate almost any garment to make it special.

A **seam** is the line where two pieces of fabric are sewn together. Instructions for sewing are on page 7. A **hem** is found along the bottom of a garment, where the fabric is turned under to make a smooth edge.

Scissors. Scissors need to be sharp to cut through fabric and cardboard. Be careful when you cut with them.

Pinking shears. This is a special scissors that cuts a zigzag line. Cutting with it will help keep the cut edge from *fraying*. Fraying is when threads pull off of the cut edge of a piece of cloth, making the edge look rough and unfinished.

Thread. Regular sewing thread is strong enough for all the projects in this book. Use a double thickness and your thread will be even stronger. To make your thread double thick, cut a long piece of thread, and push one end through the eye (hole) of a needle. Pull the two ends together and tie them in a knot. It will look like a big loop of thread. Be careful when using a sharp needle!

Use **embroidery floss** for bigger stitches and for decoration. If you want the stitches to show, then you could also use a big needle and sew with yarn.

Rope and cording. You can use many different kinds of rope and cord to make rope critters, and yarn and coil baskets. Natural fiber rope made from hemp or cotton will work better than plastic and nylon ropes. Buy rope at a hardware store; buy cording at a fabric store.

Pliers/wire cutters. You'll need a strong tool called a pliers with a wire cutter to cut the wire when you make some of the projects in this book. A scissors is not strong enough. Ask an adult to help you work safely with any sharp tool.

Crepe paper. Crepe paper is thin, colored streamers sold at dime stores and party stores in rolls. Crepe paper is commonly used to decorate for birthday parties.

Plaster of Paris. This is a powder you can buy at a hardware store or art supply store. You mix it with water to make a white plaster that dries hard.

Clay. A recipe for making sculpting dough is on page 18. You can also buy different kinds of clay at craft and art supply stores. Some dry in the open air, others require baking, and others stay soft so you can reuse them.

Part One: Make Crafts!

A Note to Grown-Ups

Make Crafts! features twenty-five unique craft projects plus numerous variations that will fire the imagination of boys and girls ages six to eleven. The projects are open-ended: Kids learn techniques they can use to produce handcrafts of their own design.

By inviting kids to adapt traditional folk art techniques, *Make Crafts!* encourages individual creativity. Children will create beautiful crafts that can be used and admired every day: colorful handwoven baskets, contemporary jewelry, frames, toys and games. Kids will get to work with fabric, rope, wood, clay, leather, papier-maché, metal, and other familiar craft materials. They'll get valuable experience in following directions, planning, creative problem solving, and seeing a project through to completion. They'll work on tactile skills such as weaving and pounding. They'll work on fine motor skills, too, such as gluing and stitching. And at the same time, they'll have an opportunity to express themselves creatively and produce something that will win them praise and boost their self-confidence.

Getting the Most Out of the Projects

While the projects provide clear step-by-step instructions and photographs, feel free to substitute and improvise. The list of materials at the beginning of each activity is for the featured project only. Suggested alternatives may require different supplies. Again, kids are encouraged to substitute and use whatever materials they have access to (and permission to use!). The projects offer flexibility to make it easy for you and your child to try as many activities as you wish.

All of the projects can be done with household items or inexpensive, easy-to-find supplies. Here are some items you'll want to make sure you have on hand: rope, thin wire, paper grocery bags, corrugated cardboard, paper plates, newspaper, scrap cloth, ribbons and yarn, wire coat hangers, old leather items, containers made of #6 recyclable plastic, aluminum foil and plastic sandwich bags.

How to Sew

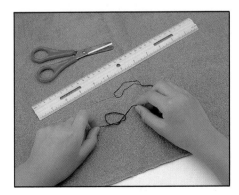

1 Cut a piece of thread about 24″ (61cm) long and poke it through the eye of a needle. Pull the ends even and tie a knot.

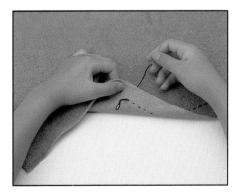

2 Sew with small stitches in and out of your fabric. Check each stitch to be sure your thread hasn't tangled underneath.

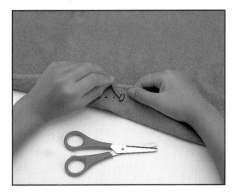

3 After you've stitched awhile, the thread will get short. Push the needle to the back of your work, make a knot, and cut the thread.

Rope Critters

Fiber Art

It's easy to make creatures with rope, wire and string. And you can really play with them when you're done! The wire lets them stand up and bend any way you want them to. We'll show you how to make a horse. Start with three pieces of rope and three pieces of wire, each 15″ (38 cm) long. Then use your imagination to create other rope animals and dolls.

Materials needed:

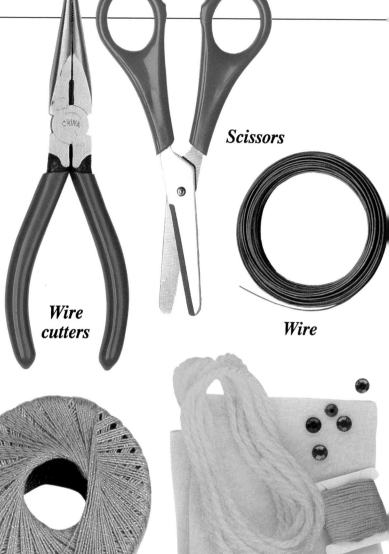

Wire cutters

Scissors

Wire

Rope ¼ ″ (½ cm) thick

String

Decorations

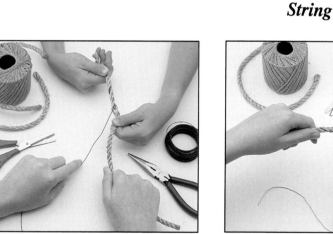

1 Twist wire into each piece of rope. Try to hide the wire inside the twists. It's easier if someone holds one end of the rope for you.

2 Make a loop and tie it tight with string. This is the horse's head. Tie the other two pieces of rope onto the body to make four legs.

3 Pull apart the fibers of the rope to make a fringe tail. Cut the wire out of the tail. Tie string tightly around the bottoms of the legs.

Glue short pieces of fringed rope to the neck to make a mane. If you want to, you can dress your rope horse with a ribbon halter and bright felt saddle blanket.

One long rope bent and wrapped with string creates this doll's head and neck. Another rope is tied on above the waist to make her arms. Then the rope is unraveled below the arms to make a fluffy skirt.

Use your imagination to make any animal you choose. Glue decorations onto the rope, or color the rope with felt-tip pens.

Weather Vanes

Papier-Maché

Weather vanes are made of wood or metal. They're flat so they can spin and show the direction of the wind. What weather vanes have you seen on the tops of old buildings? You can build a *replica*, or model, of a weather vane to decorate a room in your house.

Plaster of Paris, water and bowl

Materials needed:

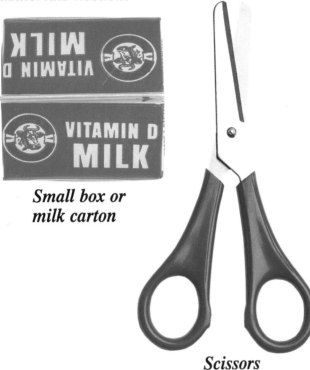

Small box or milk carton

Scissors

Acrylic paint or colored markers

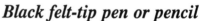

Black felt-tip pen or pencil

Craft knife

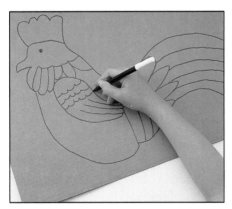

1 Draw a character for your weather vane on the cardboard. Make a traditional weather vane, like this rooster, or design your own.

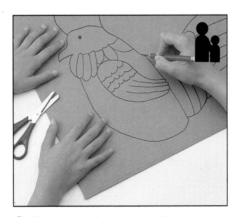

2 Cut your shape out of the cardboard. Use a strong scissors or ask an adult to help you cut with a sharp craft knife.

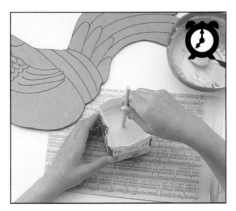

3 Make plaster following the directions on the box. Pour it into the carton. Stick the dowel in and wait for the plaster to harden.

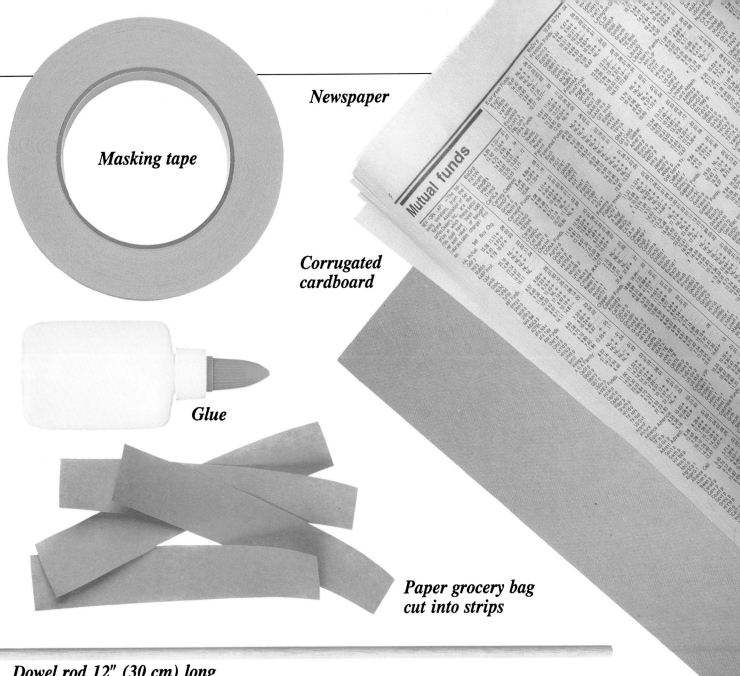

Masking tape

Newspaper

Corrugated cardboard

Glue

Paper grocery bag cut into strips

Dowel rod 12" (30 cm) long

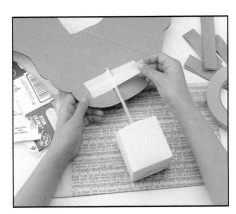

4 Tear away the box from the hard plaster base. Tape the back of the weather vane character to the top of the dowel rod.

5 Cover all the parts of your weather vane with paper strips smeared with glue. Smooth them down. Let the glue dry overnight.

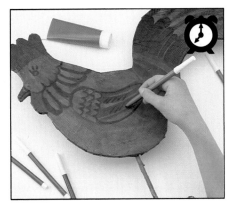

6 Paint your weather vane brown like wood or rusted metal. Let it dry. Add light colors with markers to make it look *antique*, or very old.

Weather Vanes

Here's the finished rooster weather vane.

This angel is painted black to look like wrought iron. Many weather vanes have arrows to point in the direction of the wind.

A horse is a traditional weather vane. But paint it like a zebra, and you've got an unusual work of art.

If you like building with papier-maché, try making different kinds of statues for your room or covered patio.

This whale looks like a weather vane made of copper. When copper gets old, it *tarnishes*, or turns green.

Yarn Baskets

Basketry

These soft baskets are just right for gathering eggs or holding small toys. They're so beautiful, no one will believe you made them yourself. But you can—with rope and colorful yarn or scrap cloth. Once you get the hang of it, you won't want to stop.

Materials needed:

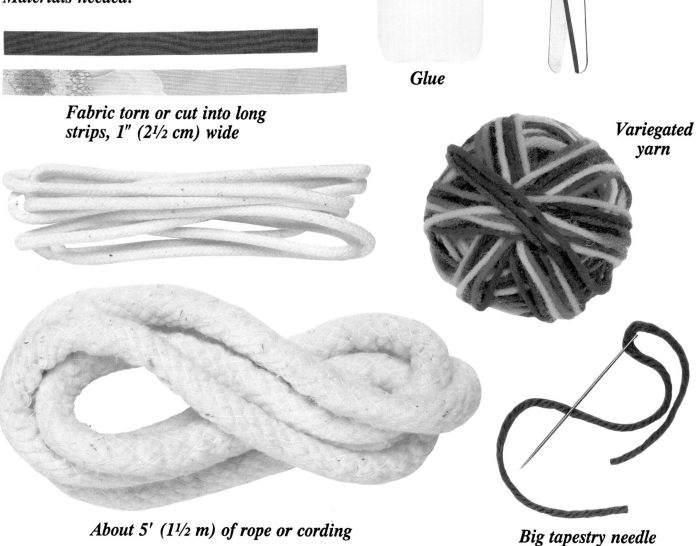

Fabric torn or cut into long strips, 1" (2½ cm) wide

Glue

Scissors

Variegated yarn

About 5' (1½ m) of rope or cording

Big tapestry needle

Ruler

1 Tie a long piece of yarn to the end of the rope. Thread the needle on the end of the yarn. Start wrapping the yarn around the rope.

2 Wrap 2″ (5 cm) of rope. Bend it into a U. Poke the needle up through the end of the rope. Wrap yarn around the outside of the U.

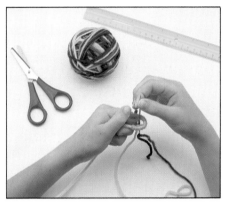

3 Wrap another 1″ (2½ cm) of rope. Curl it around the U to start a spiral. Poke the needle up through the center.

4 Pull the yarn tight. Push the needle down where the wrapped yarn ends, *in between* the two layers of rope.

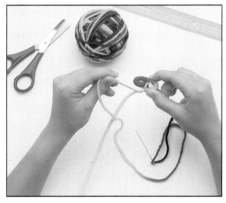

5 Come up around the outside to complete the stitch. You will make many of these stitches as you wrap and build your basket.

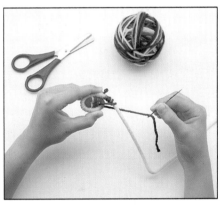

6 Keep wrapping. Every inch or so, make another stitch through the last row to pull the wrapped part in tight against the spiral.

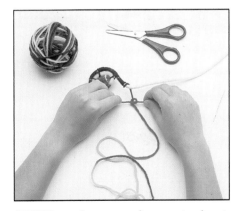

7 When the yarn piece gets short, take the needle off and tie a new piece of yarn onto the short piece. Thread the needle on the new end.

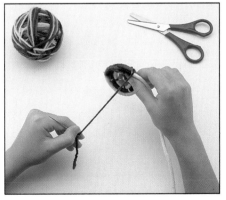

8 When your spiral is 3″ (8 cm) across, make the sides go up. Set the newly wrapped rope *on top* of the spiral, and stitch it tight.

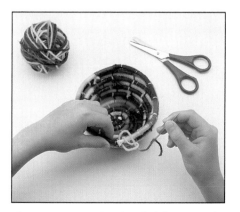

9 When your basket is big enough, trim the end of the rope. Wrap the yarn as far as you can. Make a knot, and stitch it to the basket.

Coil Baskets

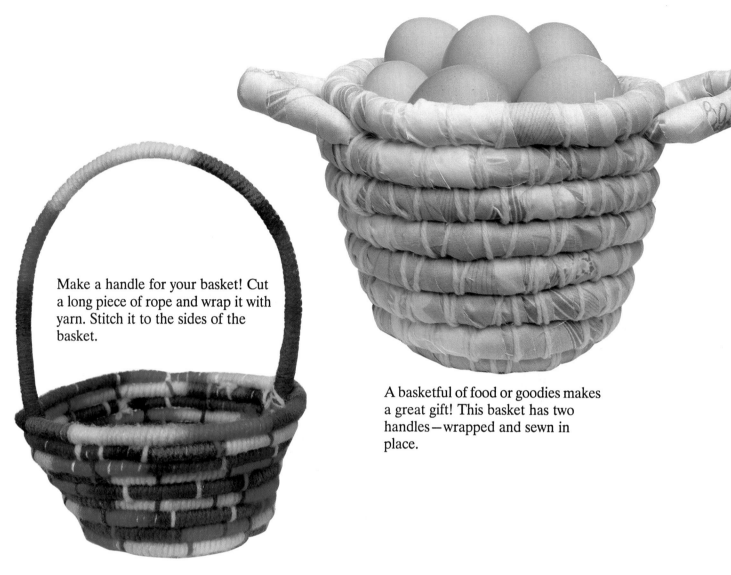

Make a handle for your basket! Cut a long piece of rope and wrap it with yarn. Stitch it to the sides of the basket.

A basketful of food or goodies makes a great gift! This basket has two handles—wrapped and sewn in place.

Rag Basket

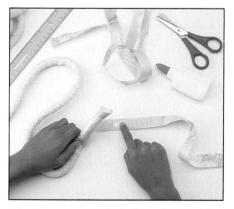

1 Cut cotton cloth into long, thin strips. Wrap these around a 5′ (1½ m) piece of rope. Spread glue on the strips as you wrap.

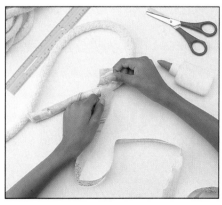

2 When you get to the last 2″ (5 cm) of a rag strip, place a new strip under it. Wrap them together, and then continue wrapping the new strip.

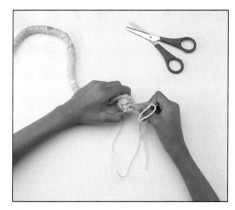

3 Keep adding strips until the whole rope is covered. Now coil the rope and use the stitch with yarn as shown in steps 2 to 5 on page 15 to make a basket.

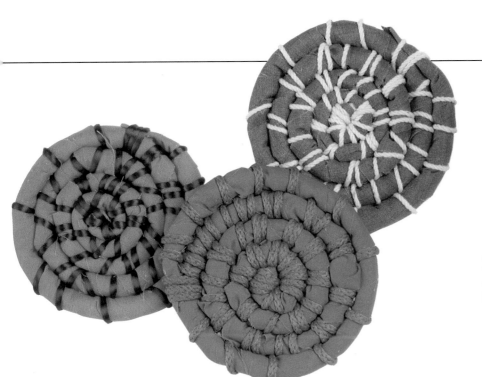

It's easy to make a set of coasters! Just keep building your flat spiral bigger and bigger, without any sides.

After you finish making your balloon basket and it's dry, you can add more glue where pieces of yarn and ribbon touch each other. Let the glue dry, and your basket will be even stronger.

Balloon Basket

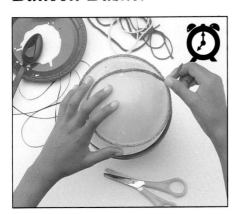

1 Dip pieces of yarn and ribbon in glue and wrap them around a blown-up balloon. Wrap in all different directions. Let the glue dry overnight.

2 After the glue has dried, pop the balloon and peel it away from the yarn pieces. Trim around the top of your basket.

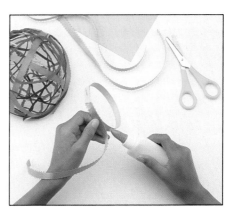

3 Make a base: Cut a strip of heavy paper. Staple it to make a ring. Glue ribbon around it. Squeeze glue along the top edge and set the basket on top.

Jointed Puppets

Working With Clay

You'll love these silly dancing puppets! Make the puppets with either homemade sculpting dough or store-bought clay. Store-bought clay often has to be baked to get hard; follow the directions on the box.

For sculpting dough: Mix 1½ cups of white flour, 1½ cups salt, 1 tablespoon of oil and enough water to make a smooth, soft clay (about ½ cup). If the dough gets too sticky while you work with it, add a little more flour. Store in plastic in the refrigerator. It will dry hard if you leave it out overnight. Or, you can bake it in a low-temperature oven (250°F) for an hour or so.

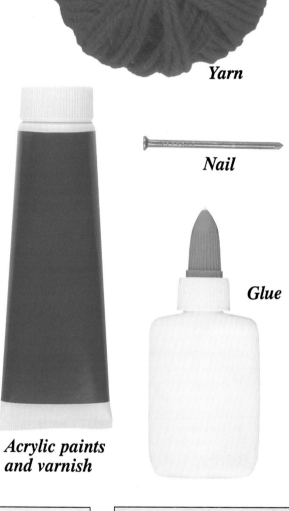

Yarn

Nail

Glue

Materials needed:

Food coloring or felt-tip pens

Acrylic paints and varnish

1 Shape a body and head out of dough. Pinch the shoulders out wide. Add bits of dough to make the face and clothes.

2 Use smaller chunks of dough to shape the arms and legs. Use toothpicks to carve details into each piece.

3 Poke a hole through the top of each arm and leg; shoulders and hips, too. Make each hole smooth and not too close to the edge.

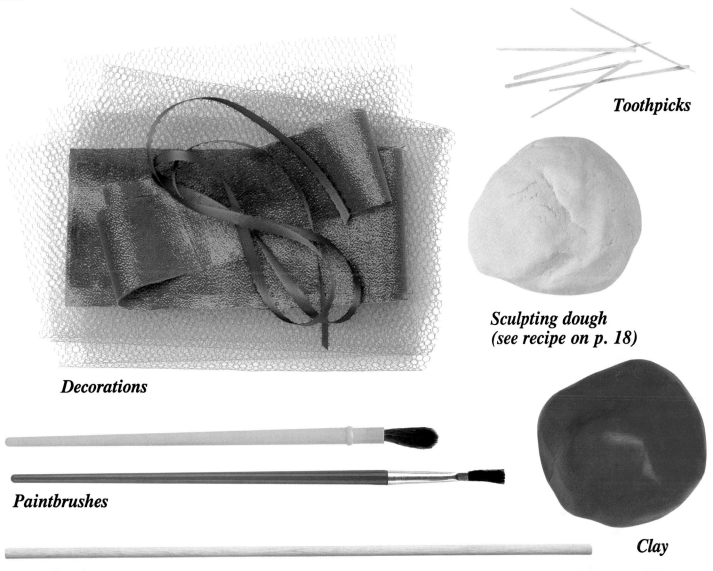

Toothpicks

**Sculpting dough
(see recipe on p. 18)**

Decorations

Paintbrushes

Clay

Dowel rod

4 Hold the puppet with one hand and *gently* twist the dowel rod up into its back. Take the dowel out if you bake your puppet.

5 Bake or air-dry a dough puppet; bake a clay puppet. If you took the dowel out to bake it, glue it back in when the puppet is cool.

6 Paint your puppet and let it dry. Add a coat of clear acrylic varnish. Let the varnish dry, and tie the pieces together with yarn.

Clay Puppets

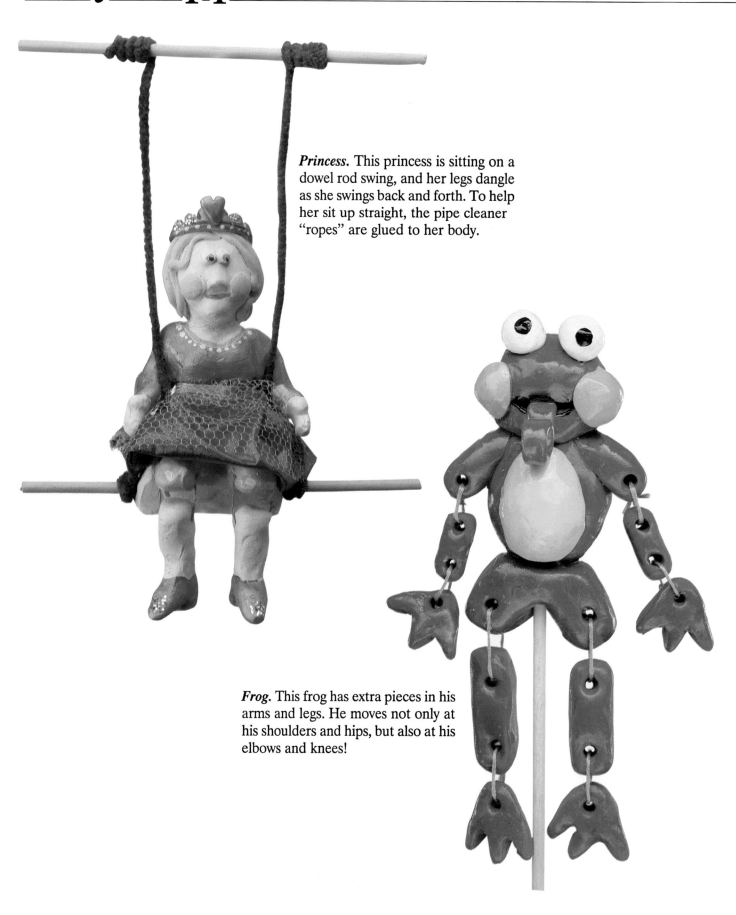

Princess. This princess is sitting on a dowel rod swing, and her legs dangle as she swings back and forth. To help her sit up straight, the pipe cleaner "ropes" are glued to her body.

Frog. This frog has extra pieces in his arms and legs. He moves not only at his shoulders and hips, but also at his elbows and knees!

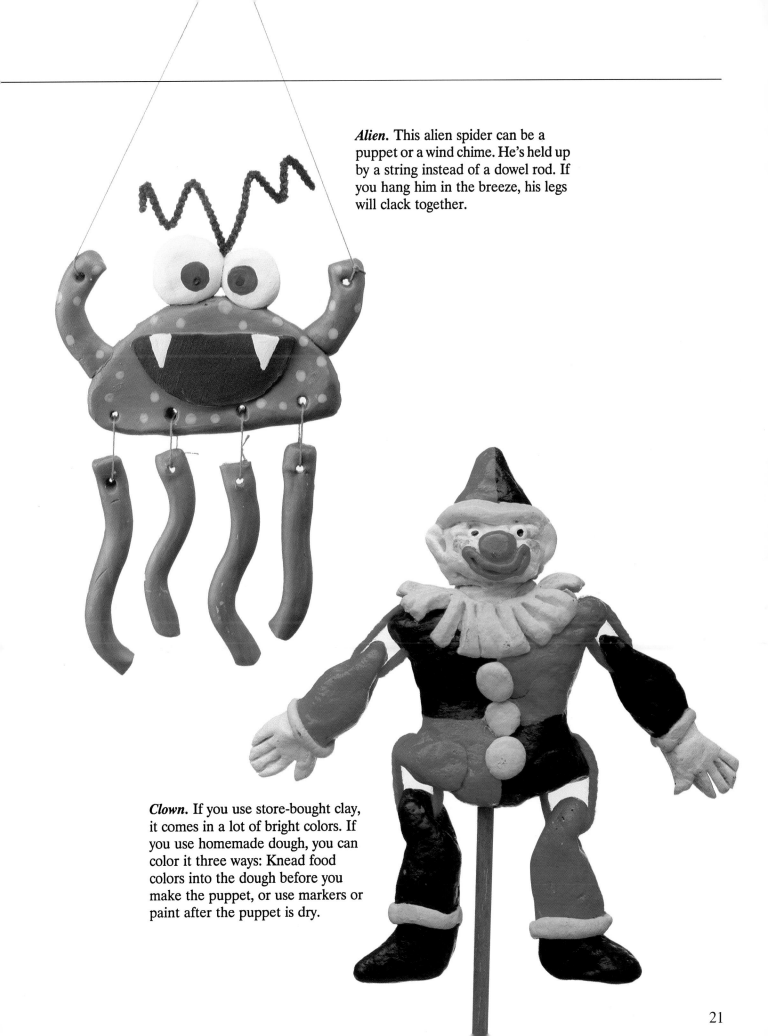

Alien. This alien spider can be a puppet or a wind chime. He's held up by a string instead of a dowel rod. If you hang him in the breeze, his legs will clack together.

Clown. If you use store-bought clay, it comes in a lot of bright colors. If you use homemade dough, you can color it three ways: Knead food colors into the dough before you make the puppet, or use markers or paint after the puppet is dry.

Frameworks

Making Wooden Frames

A beautiful wooden frame you make yourself can turn any picture into a work of art. Save the sticks from frozen treats or buy a bag of craft sticks at a craft store. You can even collect twigs and use them to build your frame.

Sandpaper

Materials needed:

Glue

Craft knife

Paintbrush

Sticks

Paint

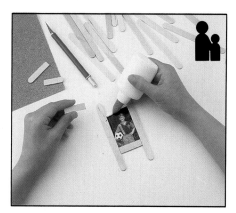

1 Glue sticks on the sides of your photo. Have an adult cut sticks to fit across the top and bottom. Sand the ends smooth, then glue them in place.

2 Glue sticks across the top and bottom, on top of the side sticks. They should overlap the first layer of sticks you cut.

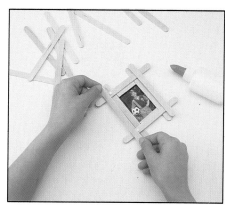

3 Glue two more sticks along the sides, then two more on the top and bottom. Keep building up and out until you get to the end of the sticks.

When you've built layers as far as you can go, let the glue dry overnight. Then decorate your frame with paint and little toys.

Build a frame with natural sticks! Have an adult help cut a lot of twigs the same size with a pruning clipper. Glue your photo onto cardboard. Then add sticks following steps 2 and 3. Use a lot of glue wherever the sticks touch each other. Be careful not to get glue on the photo.

Weaving

Weaving With Cloth and Paper

On the next six pages, you'll see how to weave a heart basket, a star ornament, and two kinds of place mats. You can use cloth or paper. It's fun to use colored paper, like wallpaper or wrapping paper. The best part about making woven creations is *using* them or giving them to a friend.

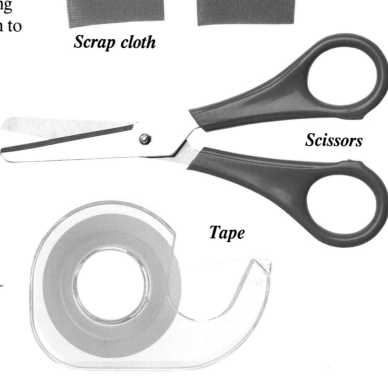

Scrap cloth

Materials needed:

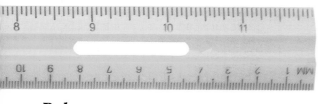

Ruler

Scissors

Tape

Pencils

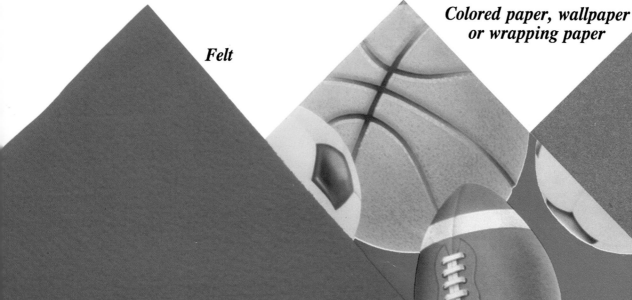

Felt

Colored paper, wallpaper or wrapping paper

Clear, sticky shelf paper

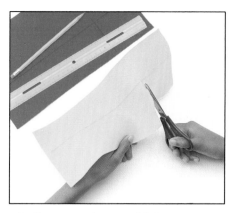

1 Cut two pieces of felt or paper 3″ by 9″ (8 cm by 24 cm). We show red and yellow felt here. Fold the pieces in half.

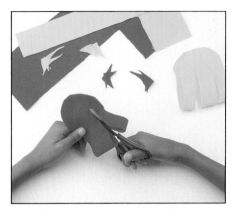

2 Trim the unfolded ends so they're round. Cut two slits in each piece, 3″ (8 cm) long, up from the folded end.

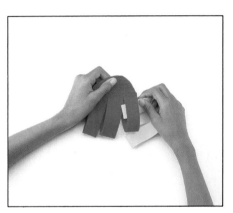

3 Now you're ready to start weaving. Slip a yellow strip *through* a red one.

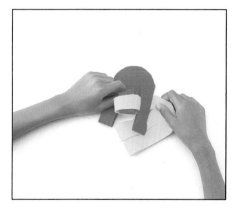

4 Push the middle red strip *through* the yellow one. Then put the yellow strip *inside* the last red one.

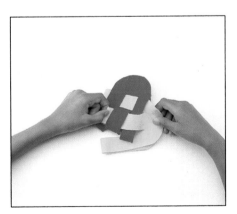

5 Do just the opposite for the second strip: red through yellow, then yellow through red, then red through yellow.

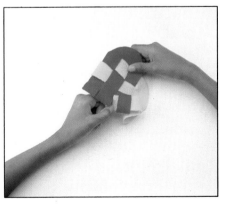

6 Now repeat steps 3 and 4 with the last yellow strip. Pull the felt gently, and you've made a heart shape!

Weaving Hearts and Stars

Turn your woven heart into a basket by gluing a strip of felt from front to back—on the inside—to make a handle.

It's easiest to learn how to make a star if you start with the same colors used in the steps on the next page. Once you get the hang of it, you can use any colors you want. Try using wrapping paper or colorful pages from magazines.

This heart basket is made of shiny paper. Cutting the strips different sizes really changes the way the finished weaving looks!

Cover strips of paper with sticky shelf paper that looks like wood to make a traditional ornament from *Scandanavia* (a region in Europe). Use a needle and thread to poke a small hole in the star, and make a loop of thread to hang it by.

1 Cut four strips of paper 1″ (2½ cm) wide and 22″ (56 cm) long. Tape two pieces together if you need to. Fold each strip in half, and cut the ends into points.

2 Place the red strip sideways. Fold the green strip over the red one, pointing down. Fold blue (or purple!) over green. Fold yellow over blue. Tuck yellow inside red.

3 Push the strips together to make a square. Now fold one side of each strip back over the square in this order: yellow, blue, green, red. Weave red under yellow.

4 Bend the top green strip forward, then over to the side. Pinch the paper so it makes a triangle.

5 Twist the green strip around to the back, then down over the front. Weave it under the red strip in the square. Pull it snug, and squeeze it to make a point.

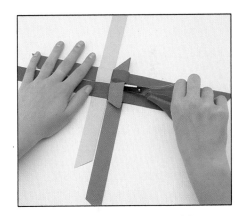

6 Trim the green strip so it's even with the bottom of the red strip it's tucked under.

7 Now repeat the action in steps 4 to 6 with the red strip at the left.

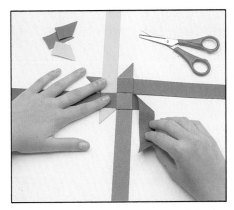

8 Now repeat steps 4 to 6 with the yellow strip at the bottom. Then do the blue strip at the right. Turn the star over.

9 Do steps 4 to 6 with each strip in this order: yellow, red, green, blue. When the blue strip is folded and trimmed, you're done!

Weaving Place Mats

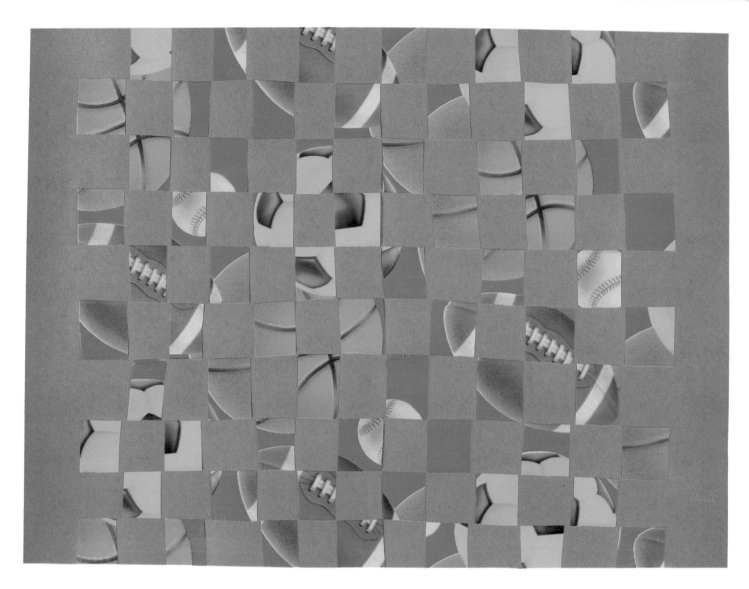

Paper

1 Fold a big piece of construction paper in half. Cut slits in from the fold. Don't cut all the way to the end! Leave 1″ (2½ cm) uncut.

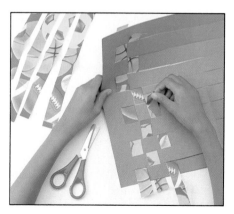

2 Cut 1″ (2½ cm) paper strips long enough to go from top to bottom of the construction paper. Weave the strips through the slits.

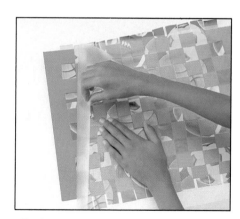

3 Cover both sides of the weaving with clear, sticky shelf paper. Smooth it down and trim the sides even.

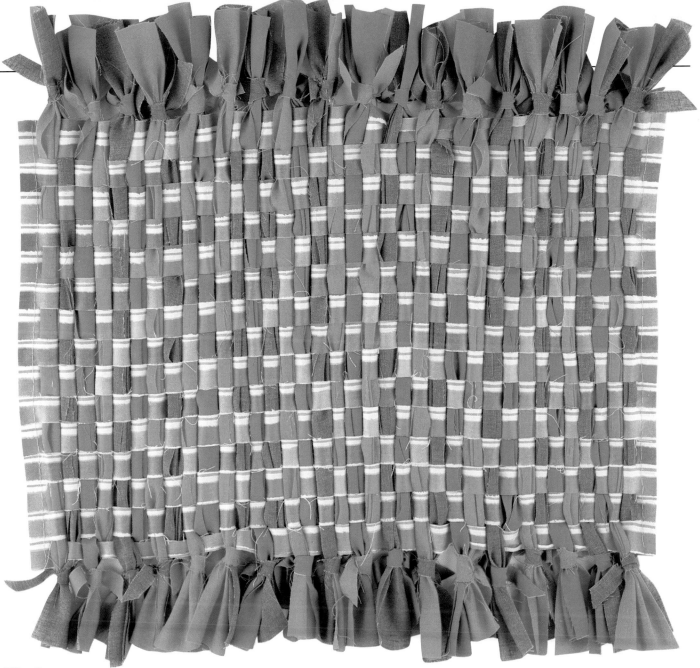

Cloth

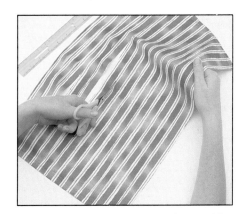

1 Cut a cloth 12″ (30 cm) by 18″ (46 cm) and sew around the edges. Cut slits from side to side. Leave ½″ (2 cm) uncut on each side.

2 Cut 30 strips of cloth 2″ (5 cm) wide and 16″ (40 cm) long. Weave these strips into the slits. Push them snug against each other.

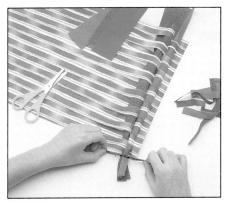

3 Fix the strips so there are 2″ (5 cm) above and 2″ (5 cm) below the mat. Tie every two strips together with a smaller strip.

Wind Fish

Building With Cloth

Every spring, Japanese children make wind fish to celebrate Children's Day. They hang the colorful cloth fish outdoors to flap and wiggle in the breeze. They look like fish swimming up a river. The traditional wind fish look like a kind of fish called *carp*, but you can make one that looks like a serpent or dragon or shark or any kind of fish you want. It's good luck to have a wind fish, and it's fun to make one of your own.

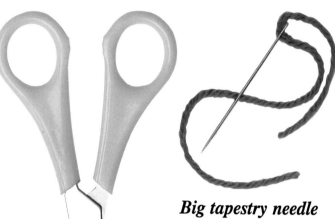

Cloth 24" (61 cm) by 36" (91 cm) or longer

Materials needed:

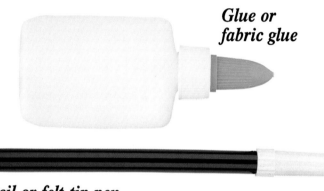

Glue or fabric glue

Pencil or felt-tip pen

Scissors

Big tapestry needle

Ruler

String

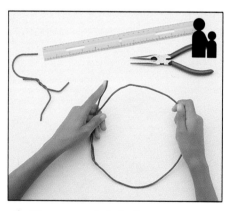

1 Have an adult help you cut an 18" (46 cm) length of wire and bend it into a circle with the pliers.

2 Fold your cloth in half lengthwise. Draw the side of a fish or serpent and cut it out. Cut both layers of cloth, but not the folded edge.

3 Spread glue along the inside of the cut edge, all the way up the side. Pinch the two layers together. Let the glue dry overnight.

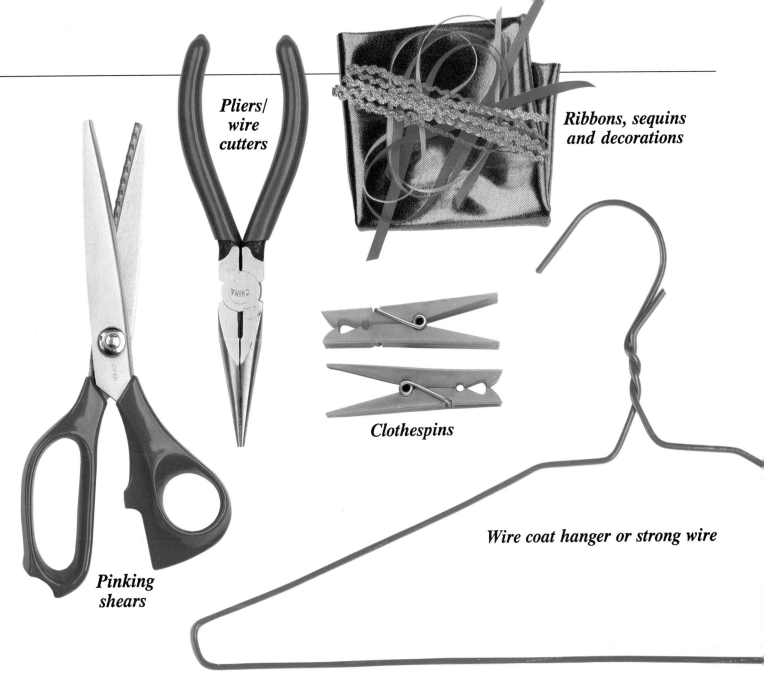

Pliers/ wire cutters

Ribbons, sequins and decorations

Clothespins

Pinking shears

Wire coat hanger or strong wire

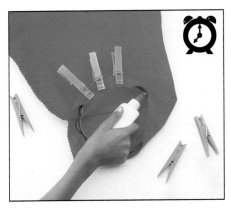

4 Put the wire circle in the opening at the top. Fold some cloth over the wire and glue it to the inside. Put clothespins on and let the glue dry.

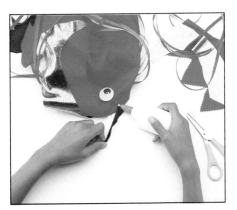

5 Paint your fish or add scraps of colorful cloth and ribbon. Use buttons for eyes. Add glitter, sequins, or whatever kinds of decorations you like.

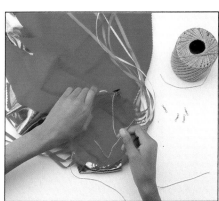

6 Cut three pieces of string, each 12″ (30 cm) long. Use the needle to poke each one through the cloth and tie it around the wire circle.

Wind Fish

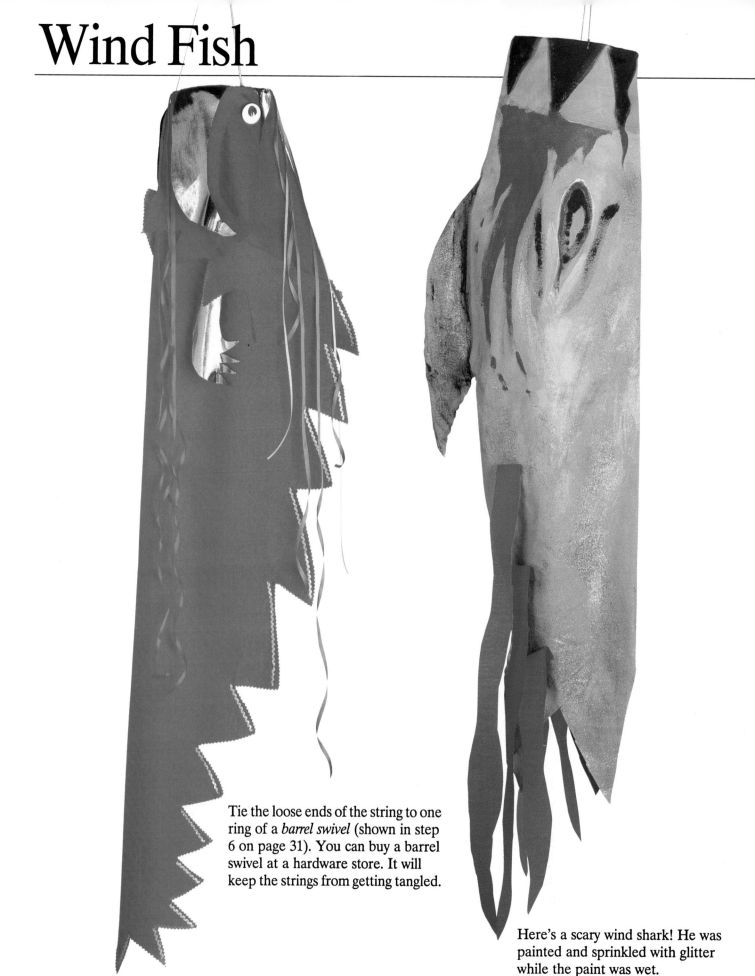

Tie the loose ends of the string to one ring of a *barrel swivel* (shown in step 6 on page 31). You can buy a barrel swivel at a hardware store. It will keep the strings from getting tangled.

Here's a scary wind shark! He was painted and sprinkled with glitter while the paint was wet.

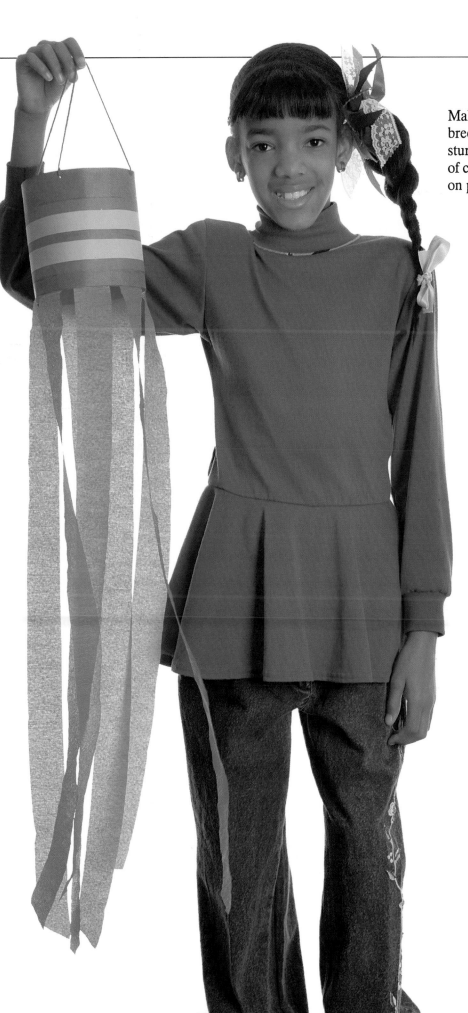

Making a paper wind sock is a breeze! Cut and staple a loop of sturdy paper. Attach long streamers of crepe paper. Add yarn as in step 6 on page 31.

Checkerboard

Woodworking

Checkers is an all-time favorite game, and it's twice as much fun when you play on a game board you make yourself! Buy the wood pieces at a hardware or lumber store. Ask if a clerk can cut the exact pieces you need. Or ask an adult to help you saw the wood. You'll need a 13″ by 20″ (33 cm by 51 cm) piece of plywood that's ¼″ to ½″ thick. And you'll need four pieces of ¾″ wide shelf edging, two that are 20″ (51 cm) long and two that are 13½″ (34 cm) long.

Materials needed:

Sandpaper

Dishes for holding paints

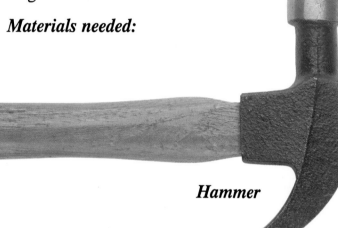
Hammer

Acrylic paints

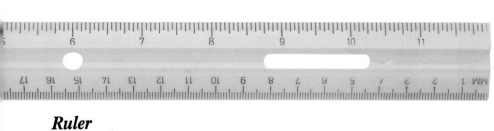
Ruler

Pencil

Paintbrushes

Newspaper

Plywood

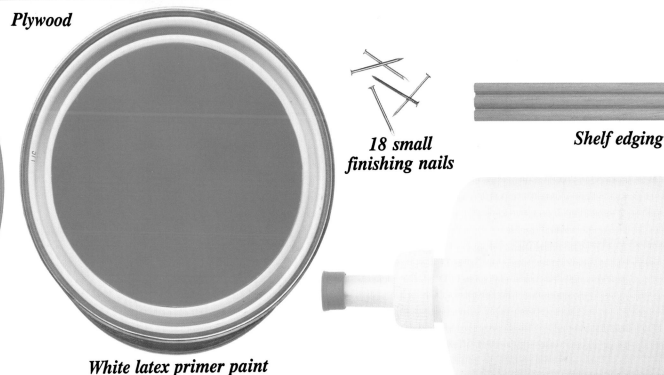

18 small finishing nails

Shelf edging

White latex primer paint

Carpenter's glue

Building the Checkerboard

1 Rub the cut edges of the wood pieces with sandpaper. Also rub the surface of the plywood that will be the top of your checkerboard.

2 Attach the long side strips to the plywood first, then the shorter ends. For each piece, squeeze glue along the edge of the plywood.

3 Have an adult set an edging strip into the glue and hold it while you nail it down. Use five nails on the long sides and four on the short ends.

Checkerboards

Paint colorful designs on each end of your checkerboard. Then have an adult help you add a final coat of varnish to protect your work. Make twenty-four checkers out of clay or sculpting dough (see recipe on page 18). Paint twelve a light color and twelve a dark color, and you're ready to play!

Painting the Checkerboard

4 After the glue has dried for an hour or more, paint the whole tray with white latex primer paint. Set it aside to dry overnight.

5 Draw a 12″ by 12″ (30 cm by 30 cm) *grid*. Make eight rows of eight squares that have 1½″ (4 cm) sides. Ask for help if you need it.

6 Paint over the grid with a light color mixed with a little water. The paint should be thin enough so you can see your lines through it.

You can make a cardboard game, too. Glue a piece of white poster board on top of a piece of corrugated cardboard. Color your design with markers or paint. Collect things to be the checkers. If you play with something that you can't stack, such as stones, paint a tiny crown on one side for the kings.

7 Paint *around* the grid and all the rest of the tray with a dark color. Let the paint dry.

8 Make a checkerboard pattern with dark squares like this. Follow the lines of your grid. Paint the squares as straight as you can.

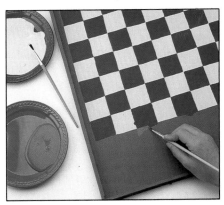

9 When the paint is dry, you can fix any places that look uneven. Carefully paint over them with the color you need to cover the "goof."

Rag Bear

Doll-Making

This terrific teddy bear might become your best friend. Or maybe you'll make one of its rag doll pals. They're easy to put together with fabric glue and scraps of colorful cotton cloth.

Materials needed:

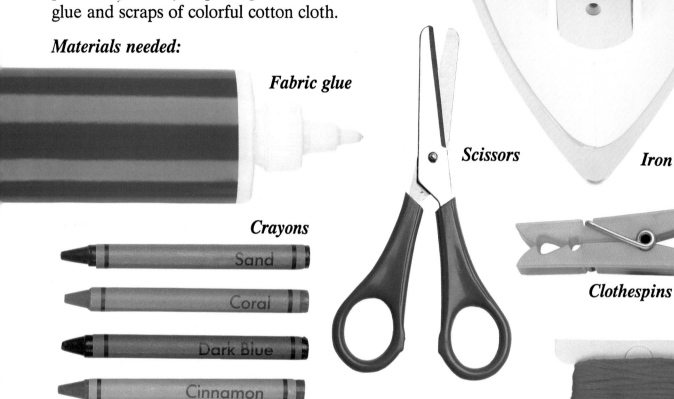

Fabric glue

Scissors

Iron

Crayons

Sand

Coral

Dark Blue

Cinnamon

Clothespins

Cloth

Red embroidery floss, ribbon and buttons (optional)

Needle

Foil and fiberfill (from a sewing store)

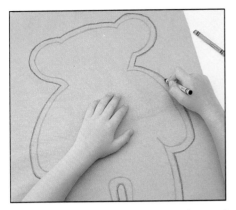

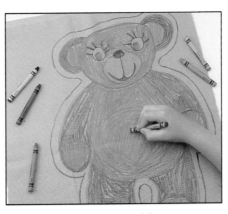

1 Draw a teddy bear on a piece of cloth. Draw a line about 1″ (2½ cm) outside of the bear. The space between the two lines is a free space.

2 Color your bear with crayons. Color the whole thing or just the details. You can make it either real or silly. Don't color the free space.

3 Ask an adult to put your bear between pieces of newspaper and iron it. Cover the iron with foil before you turn it on; set it to medium heat.

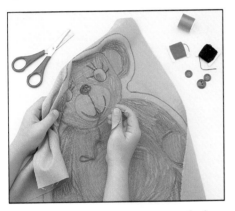

4 When it's cool, you can stitch a red mouth and add button eyes and nose. Ask an adult to help if you don't know how to sew.

5 Put your bear drawing on top of another piece of cloth. Cut around the outside line of the free space so you have two bear shapes.

6 Spread fabric glue on the free space around your bear drawing. Leave 5″ (13 cm) with no glue. Put the plain bear on top and set a heavy book on it. Let it dry.

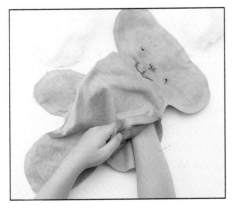

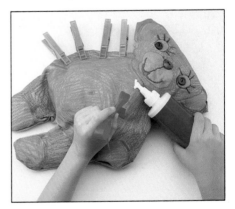

7 Carefully turn your bear right side out through the unglued opening. Stuff it with fiberfill.

8 Spread glue in the free space along the opening. Tuck the edges into the bear and squeeze it together. Put clothespins on and let the glue dry.

9 Make a ribbon bow and glue it to the bear's neck. Add any decorations you like. You can even cut out little clothes for it to wear.

Rag Pals

Here's how the finished teddy bear looks!

You can make any animal you want — just keep the outline simple. Make it with a colored cloth, or color it with crayons as shown on page 39.

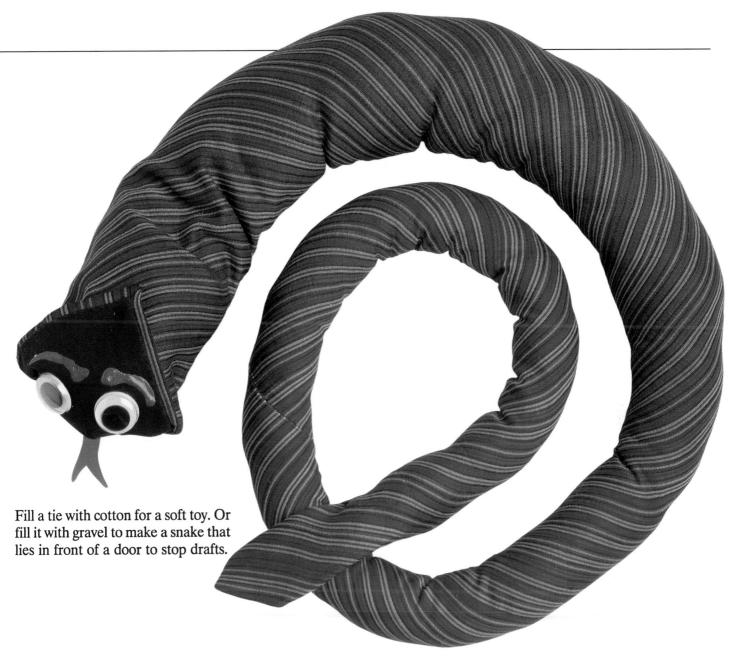

Fill a tie with cotton for a soft toy. Or fill it with gravel to make a snake that lies in front of a door to stop drafts.

Snake

1 Get permission to use an old necktie. Use fabric glue to seal the small end shut. Put a heavy book on top and let it dry overnight.

2 Stuff the necktie with cotton puffs or fiberfill from a fabric store. Use a stick or pencil to poke the stuffing way down to the end.

3 Glue the big end shut and let it dry. Then make a face with wiggly eyes, felt, fabric paint, and whatever decorations you have.

Beads

Jewelry-Making

Bright beads and crazy charms are fun to wear and simple to make. Everyone will want some of the beautiful jewelry you design! Never give your homemade jewelry to babies, though. The little pieces can be dangerous to them.

Acrylic paint and acrylic varnish

Cookie sheet and foil

Materials needed:

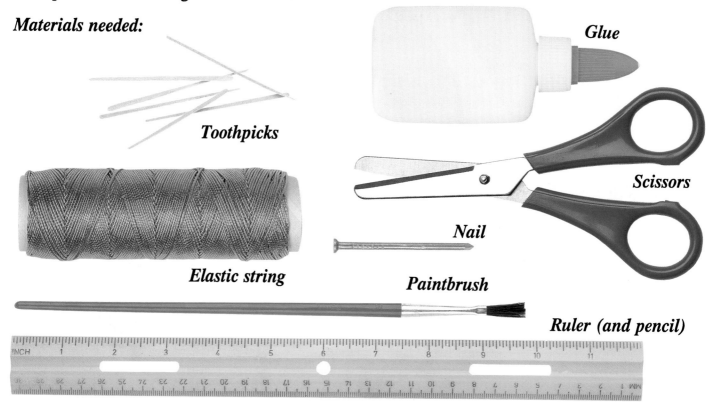

Toothpicks

Glue

Scissors

Nail

Elastic string

Paintbrush

Ruler (and pencil)

Paper Beads

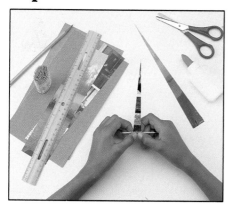

1 Cut paper into long, skinny triangles 1″ (2½ cm) wide at the bottom and 9″ (23 cm) long. Start at the wide end and roll the paper strip around a toothpick.

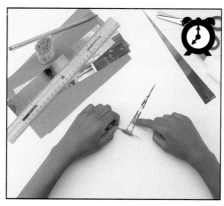

2 Spread glue on the tip. Finish rolling and press the point against the bead. Let it dry overnight, and then pull out the toothpick.

Wooden Beads

Buy wooden beads at a toy or craft store. Hold them on a nail and paint tiny designs with acrylic paints. Or color them with felt-tip pens.

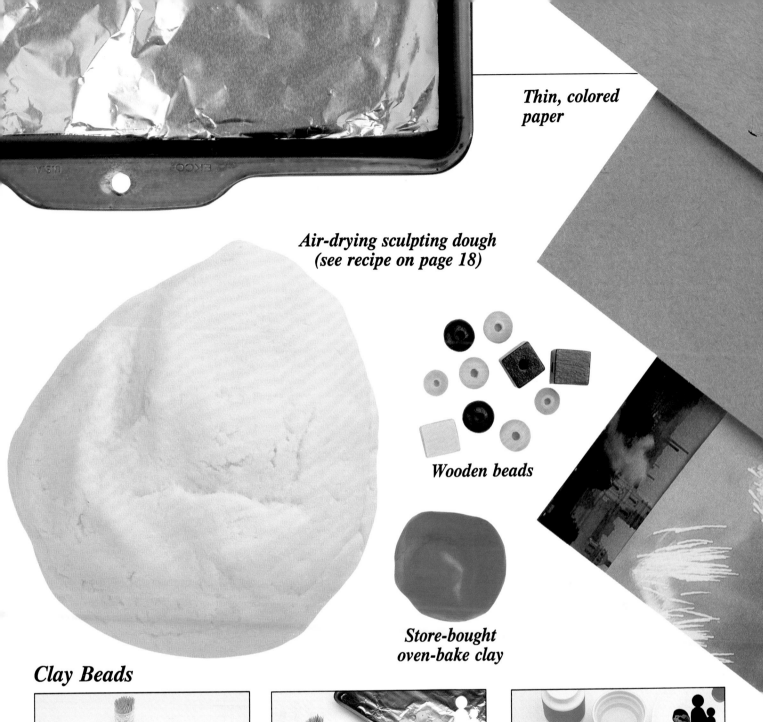

Thin, colored paper

Air-drying sculpting dough (see recipe on page 18)

Wooden beads

Store-bought oven-bake clay

Clay Beads

1 Form beads out of sculpting dough or store-bought oven-bake clay. Try making balls, cubes, disks and pyramids.

2 Push a toothpick through each bead. Set the beads on foil on a cookie sheet. Let dough beads dry; have an adult help you bake beads made of clay.

3 After the beads are hard and cool, you can paint them. Have an adult help you add a coat of acrylic varnish when the paint is dry.

Beads and Charms

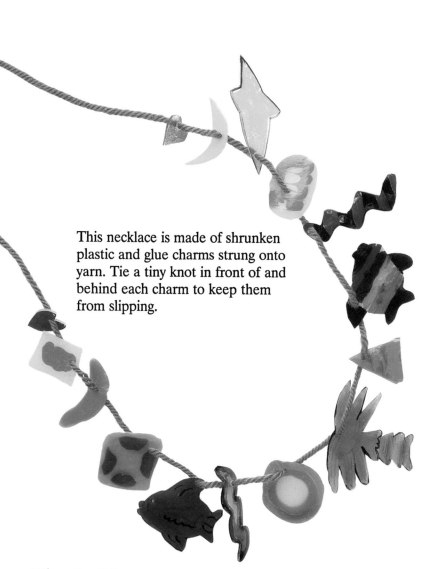

This necklace is made of shrunken plastic and glue charms strung onto yarn. Tie a tiny knot in front of and behind each charm to keep them from slipping.

Roll beads with strips of *denim* (blue jean material) instead of paper as shown on page 42. These denim beads were combined with dough beads painted red, strung on gold elastic thread from a craft store.

Safety Note ⚠️

Melting the plastic will not give off harmful gas, but fumes from burning plastic are dangerous. So watch your plastic charms carefully so they do not burn.

Plastic Charms

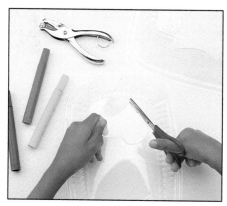

1 Cut big shapes out of shrinking plastic (from a craft store) or deli containers made out of #6 recyclable plastic.

2 Color one side of each charm with permanent markers. (Work outside or near open windows.) Punch a hole at the top. Set them on foil on a cookie sheet.

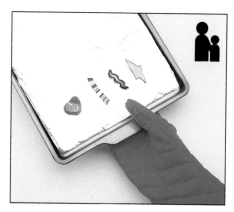

3 Have an adult help you bake the plastic in a warm oven (250°F) for three to five minutes. The charms shrink! Don't touch them until they're cool.

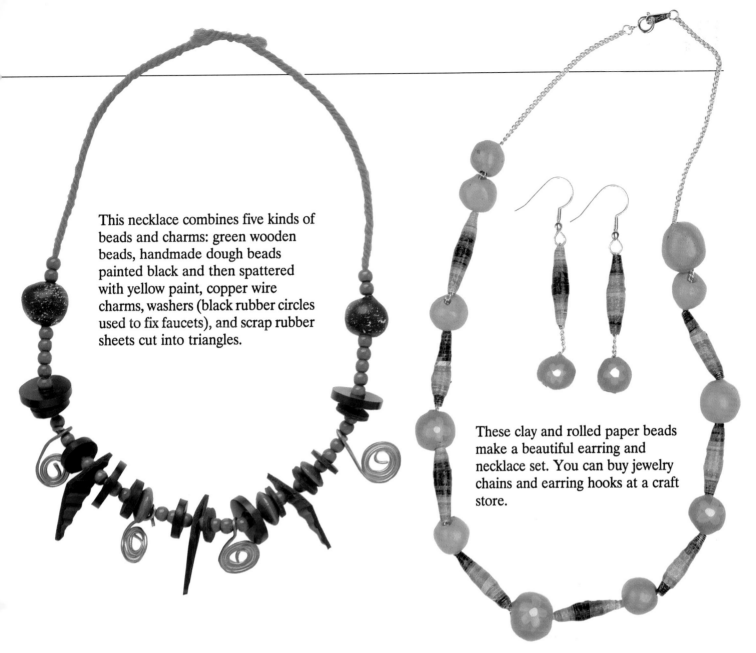

This necklace combines five kinds of beads and charms: green wooden beads, handmade dough beads painted black and then spattered with yellow paint, copper wire charms, washers (black rubber circles used to fix faucets), and scrap rubber sheets cut into triangles.

These clay and rolled paper beads make a beautiful earring and necklace set. You can buy jewelry chains and earring hooks at a craft store.

Glue Charms

1 Use store-bought colored glue or add a drop of food dye to white glue in a plastic bag. Snip a corner of the bag and squeeze the glue onto plastic wrap.

2 Let the glue charms dry overnight. Then peel them up and set them on a stack of newspaper. Pound holes into them with a small nail.

Wire Charms

Buy 20-gauge copper wire at a hardware store. Cut 4″ (10 cm) pieces with a pliers, and twist them into spirals. Bend a tiny loop at the top.

Leather Medallions

Towel

Tooled Leather

With a hammer, leather scraps and hardware pieces, you can make some great tooled leather *medallions* (small round or oval ornaments). Make one for a keychain, necklace, tree ornament or just for fun! If you have foil and an embroidery hoop, you can punch designs into metal, too (see page 48).

Hardware bits

Materials needed:

Hammer   *Nail*

Wood block

Scissors

Leather

Dish and water

1 Get permission to cut shapes out of old leather boots or purses; or use leather scraps from a shoe repair shop.

2 Wet a small towel and fold it on a dish. Slip your leather shapes between layers of wet towel and leave them overnight.

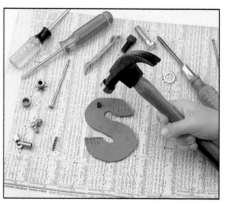

3 Set a damp leather piece on top of a stack of newspapers. Use a hammer and hardware bits to pound designs into the leather.

Here's a planet necklace.

An S-shaped ornament.

A star zipper pull.

A round keychain medallion.

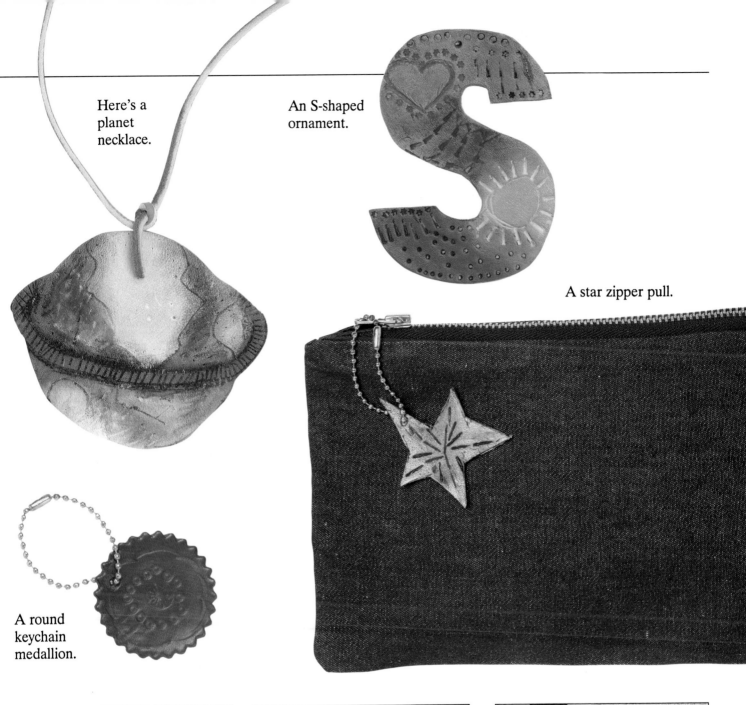

4 Scrape lines into the leather with the tip of a nail. Always be careful when using any sharp tool!

5 Pound a hole into the leather: Place it on a block of scrap wood and hammer a big nail all the way through.

6 Let the leather dry completely. Then, if you wish, ask an adult to help you rub it with shoe polish. Or use acrylic paints.

Punched Metal

Use a hammer and a nail to punch a design into the metal lid of a frozen juice can.

Keep your design simple because if you punch too many holes too close together, you won't be able to see what the picture is!

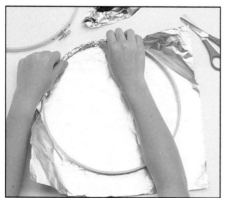

1 Tear off a piece of heavy-duty foil that is bigger than the embroidery hoop. Put the inside hoop on top of the foil and wrap it around the edges.

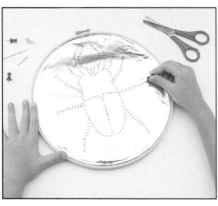

2 Put the outside hoop around the foil. Tighten the hoop. Use a small nail or push pin to gently punch holes in the foil.

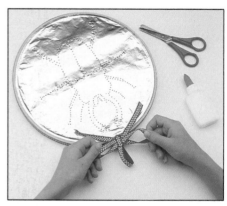

3 Glue a ribbon around the hoop and tie a big bow or make a loop. Hang the hoop from the top of the inside of a window frame.

Part Two: Make Clothes Fun!

A Note to Grown-Ups

Make Clothes Fun! features ten unique and diverse projects, plus numerous variations, for decorating clothing.

They are open-ended: kids learn techniques they can use to decorate clothes according to their own designs. The emphasis is on fun. Kids will love working with fabrics and fabric paint, sewing, weaving, embroidering, tie-dyeing, decorating with materials from buttons to lace to studs, and designing caps and team insignia patches.

Young "clothing designers" will beam when someone admires a garment they've made or decorated themselves. All the projects are kid-tested to ensure success and inspire confidence.

Getting the Most Out of the Projects

While the projects provide clear step-by-step instructions and photographs, children should feel free to substitute and improvise.

Suggested alternatives may require different supplies. Again, children are encouraged to substitute and use whatever materials they have access to (and permission to use!). The projects offer flexibility to make it easy for you and your child to try as many activities as you wish.

Here are some household items you'll want to make sure you have on hand: newspapers, scrap paper and cloth, ribbons, lace, yarn, buttons, leftover latex housepaint, soda straws, felt, beads, paper clips, string, rubber bands, safety pins, rubber gloves, plastic utensils, bucket and sponges.

Tennie Ties

Jazz up your tennis shoes with fancy shoelaces. Stripes, spots and colorful designs are easy to make with paint or markers.

Shoelaces

You must use permanent ink markers to color on shoelaces. Regular water-based felt pens will "bleed" when they get wet and could ruin your shoes. *Be careful*—permanent ink markers have a strong, bad smell. *Always get permission* and use them outside or next to an open window. Wear old clothes and work on scrap paper or newspaper.

Latex housepaint

Materials needed:

Permanent ink markers

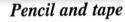
Pencil and tape

Stick

Fabric paint

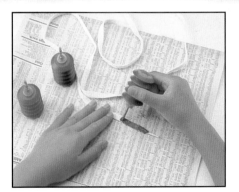

Making Stripes. Paint or draw stripes on one side—make them fat or thin, straight or slanted. When it's dry, match the colors on the other side. Try glitter paint!

Fast Stripes. Wind your shoelace tight around a pencil. Tape both ends down to hold it in place. Paint or draw long stripes of color. Leave the inside plain.

Drizzle Laces. Lay a shoelace on newspaper. Drizzle it with latex housepaint. Let it dry for one hour; then drizzle the other side.

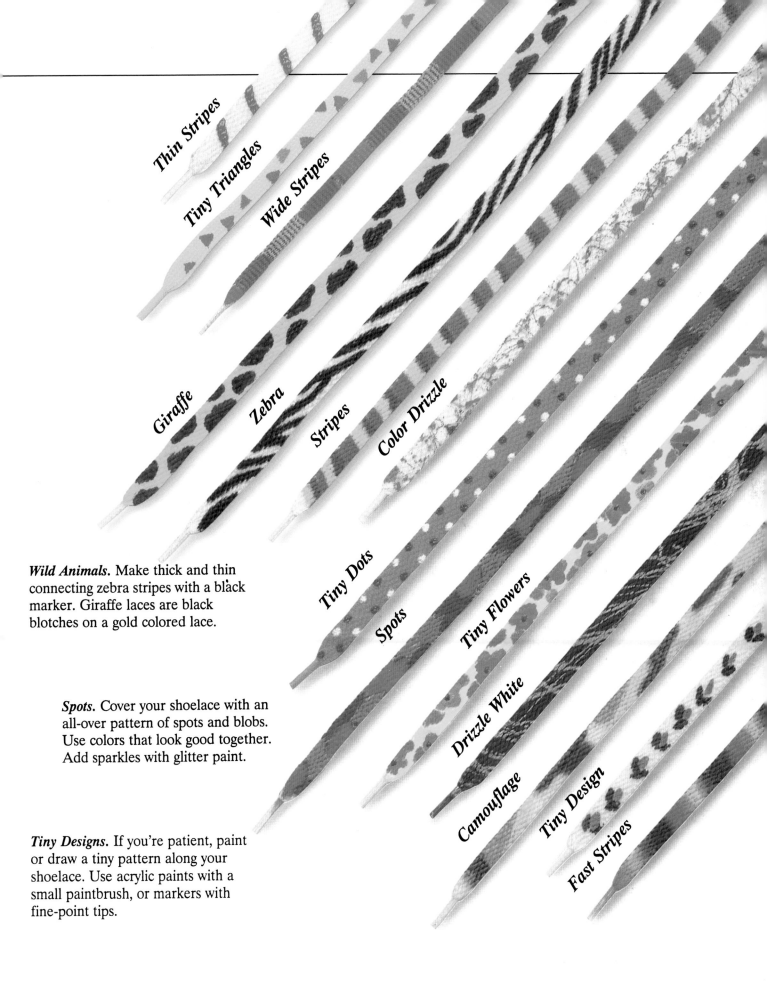

Thin Stripes

Tiny Triangles

Wide Stripes

Giraffe

Zebra

Stripes

Color Drizzle

Tiny Dots

Spots

Tiny Flowers

Drizzle White

Camouflage

Tiny Design

Fast Stripes

Wild Animals. Make thick and thin connecting zebra stripes with a black marker. Giraffe laces are black blotches on a gold colored lace.

Spots. Cover your shoelace with an all-over pattern of spots and blobs. Use colors that look good together. Add sparkles with glitter paint.

Tiny Designs. If you're patient, paint or draw a tiny pattern along your shoelace. Use acrylic paints with a small paintbrush, or markers with fine-point tips.

Painting T-Shirts

You can paint T-shirts, sweats and other clothes and turn them into colorful works of art. You'll learn several methods including drizzling or splattering paint for a wild look, or using stencils for a more careful design. Any way you choose is easy and fun and lets you express yourself on the clothes you wear!

Acrylic paint mixed with water

Latex housepaint

Scissors

Materials needed:

Scrap paper, newspaper, and tracing paper

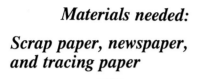

Fabric paint

Sponge pieces

Toothbrush

Masking tape

Paintbrush

Get Ready

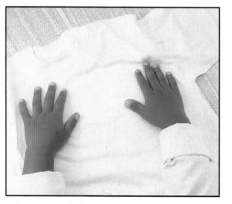

1 For drizzle, drop, and splatter, put the shirt in the bottom of a big cardboard box or on newspapers. If you don't use a box, wear old clothes!

2 Practice drizzling, dropping, and splattering paint on scrap cloth or newspaper before you work on good clothes.

3 If you use a new shirt, wash and dry it before you begin. Stuff layers of newspaper inside, and cover the neckband with paper and masking tape.

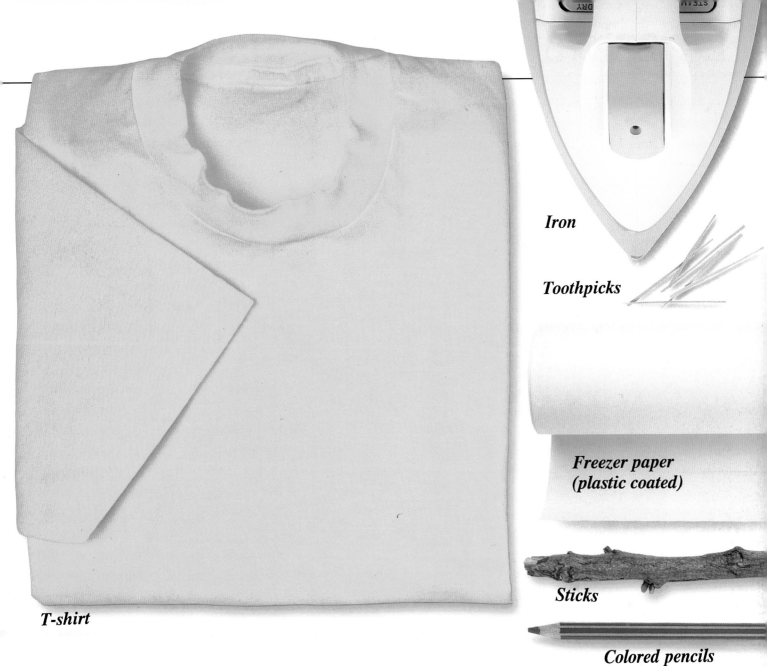

Iron

Toothpicks

**Freezer paper
(plastic coated)**

Sticks

Colored pencils

T-shirt

Drizzle

1 Dip a stick into latex paint. Pull it out and let it drip into the can for a moment. Then shake it gently over the shirt so the paint falls in a wiggly line.

2 Drizzle all over—even on the sleeves. Use one color or several colors. Let it dry for three hours, then drizzle the back of the shirt the same way.

Drip drop. Mix acrylic paints with enough water to make them runny like syrup. Use toothpicks to drip drops of paint all over the shirt.

Drizzle and Splat T-Shirts

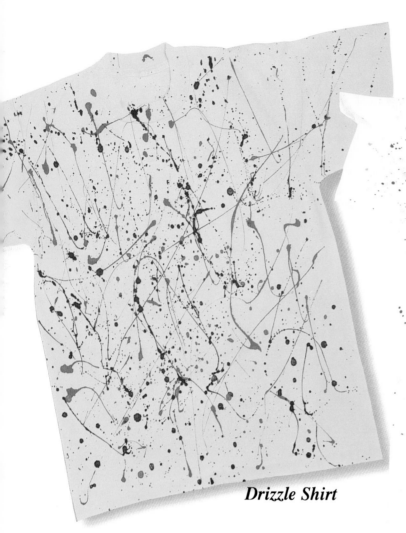

Drip Drop Shirt

Drizzle Shirt

Drizzle Shapes

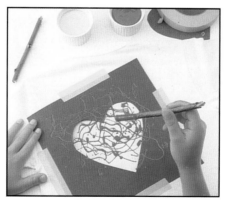

1 Cut a simple shape out of a big piece of paper. Hearts and stars, circles and fat letters are easy to start with.

2 Tape the paper stencil on the top of the shirt. Drizzle paint through the hole onto the shirt. Carefully lift the stencil to see your design below.

3 You can make several stencil shapes on one shirt—use different colors for each one! Let each layer of paint dry before putting a new stencil on top.

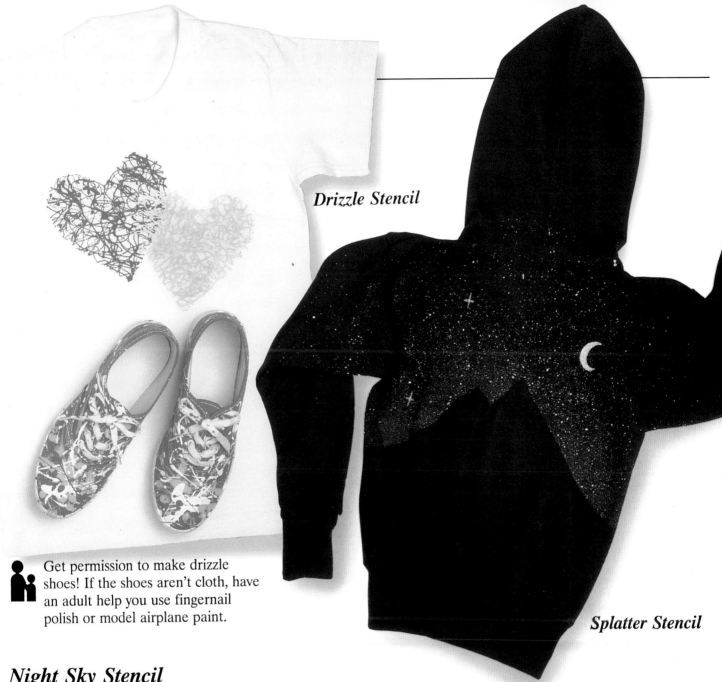

Drizzle Stencil

Splatter Stencil

Night Sky Stencil

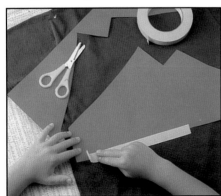

1 Make a horizon stencil. Cut mountain shapes in a large piece of paper and tape it to cover the bottom half of your shirt.

2 Dip an old toothbrush into white acrylic paint thinned with water. Rub your thumb across the bristles to splatter tiny flecks of paint all over the shirt.

3 Add flecks of light colors or glitter paint if you wish. Paint a thin crescent moon or cross-shaped stars. Let your shirt dry and remove the stencil.

Easy Stencil T-Shirts

Snowflake Stencil

Sun Stencil

Iron-On Shapes

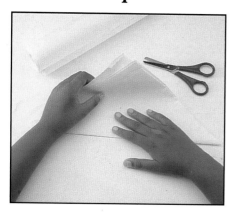

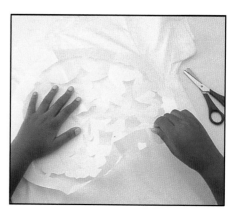

1 To make a snowflake stencil, fold a large piece of freezer wrap in half, and then in half again. Now fold that to make a triangle.

2 Use scissors to round the top. Cut zigzag or lacy holes down each side—but don't cut all the way across! Cut off the point and unfold the paper.

3 Place your snowflake stencil shiny side down on your T-shirt. Have an adult help you iron it in place. Remember to put newspaper or freezer paper inside the shirt.

Name Stencil

Word Stencil

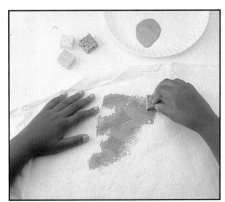

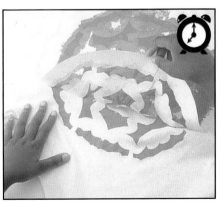

4 Put a little bit of latex or acrylic paint on a paper plate. With a sponge dab the paint onto the cloth that shows through the holes in your stencil.

5 If you use more than one color, paint each color carefully with a different sponge piece. Let the paint dry completely, then pull off the stencil.

Iron-On Words. Sketch a word or a name on the dull side of the freezer paper. Cut out the letters and iron the stencil onto your shirt. Follow Steps 3, 4 and 5.

Picture Stencil T-Shirts

1 Draw a picture on regular paper. Draw something that has interesting shapes, and use lots of colors in the different shapes.

2 Make your first stencil: Trace your drawing onto the dull side of a piece of freezer paper. Cut out all the shapes you want to be the same color.

3 Have an adult iron the stencil in place. Dab on the paint. Let it dry (use a hairdryer to speed up drying time). Pull up the stencil.

If you paint on a dark garment, use several coats of paint with each stencil so the color of the garment doesn't show through.

Cut stencils of simple shapes to make an abstract design. Let each color dry completely. The shapes can overlap if you wish.

4 Put a new piece of freezer paper over your first drawing. Make a second stencil: Trace your drawing and cut out the shapes of your second color.

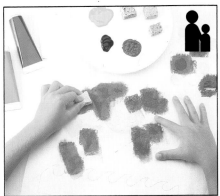

5 Lay this new stencil in place on top of what has already been painted on the shirt. Have an adult help you iron it down, then paint in the second color.

6 Let it dry, and peel up the stencil. Do this again and again for each color you want to use until you've painted the whole picture on the shirt.

Button Designs

Create a picture or design with colorful buttons. It's easy to glue or sew them on. They look best on plain, colored fabric. For light-weight clothes like T-shirts, use small buttons. Heavy things like denim, sweats and shoes can support bigger buttons. Turn your Buttons garment inside out when you wash it.

Masking tape

Materials needed:

Fabric paint

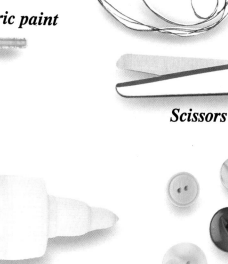
Thread and needle

Scissors

Fabric glue

Buttons

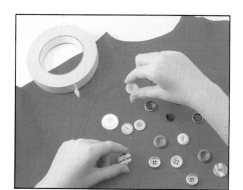

Plan a design by laying buttons on your garment and moving them around until you like what you see. Then use tape to hold them in place.

Sew. You can sew the buttons on (ask an adult for help if you need it). Lift the tape from each button as you're ready to sew it in place.

Glue. You can glue the buttons in place with fabric paint! Make a ring of paint for each button to sit in, and the color will show around the edges.

If your buttons are close together, you can move from button to button (inside the garment) without tying a knot. If your buttons are far apart, sew each one by itself. Start with a knot in your thread. After you've stitched a button, use the needle to tie a knot on the inside of the garment. Cut the thread, and make a new knot for the next button.

This butterfly was painted with black and blue fabric paint. The buttons on top make him bright and colorful.

Show Your Spirit

Support your favorite team or club—make a colorful felt patch! Design an *insignia*, or badge, for your team using your school colors or a picture of your team mascot. You can sew or glue patches on jackets, sweatshirts, gym bags or banners.

There are many kinds of fancy letters to choose from. A few styles are shown at right—try them out, or make up your own.

Materials needed:

Needle and thread

Fabric paint

Felt

Colored pencils

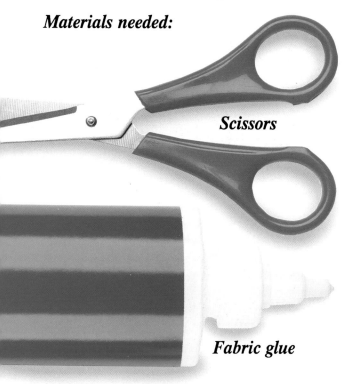

Scissors

Straight pins

Drawing paper and tracing paper

Fabric glue

1 Plan your design on paper. Draw it as big as you want the patch to be. Make a tracing of each letter and shape in your drawing.

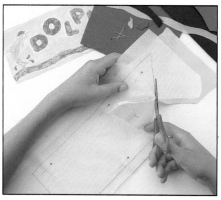

2 Lay one of the tracings on top of felt. Hold the paper in place with straight pins. Use it as a pattern to cut out the letters and shapes.

3 Cut out all the pieces. Then put them together following your design. Spread glue all over the back of each piece. Glue them down one at a time.

AABCDEFGHI
JKKLMNOPQ
RRSTUVWXYZ

ABCDEFGHIJKLMN
OPQRSTUVWXYZ

ABCDEFGHIJKLM
NOPQRSTUVWXYZ

4 Instead of cutting out the tiny inside of a letter, you can cut the shape of the hole out of the background color. Glue the hole shape *on top of* the letter.

5 Use fabric paint to draw on your patch. Add details and highlights with light colors. Be very careful, because you can't change it if you make a mistake!

6 If you put your patch on a garment you will wash, have an adult help you sew around each piece of your patch. Then sew the patch onto your garment.

Team Spirit

Once you design an insignia, like this one for a swim team called the Dolphins, you can use it over and over again on banners, caps and T-shirts.

This design was painted on a white iron-on patch with fabric paint. The paint comes in a tube with a small opening so it's easy to draw with. Iron-on patches are available at fabric and craft stores.

Here's a design for an art club, glued onto a tote bag for art supplies!

Soda Straw Weavings

Weave beautiful, colorful belts and things on a "loom" you make yourself. It's easy! Best of all, your woven creations will look so good, no one will believe you made them with soda straws!

Materials needed:

Yarn

6 plastic straws

Scissors

Ruler

6 rubber bands

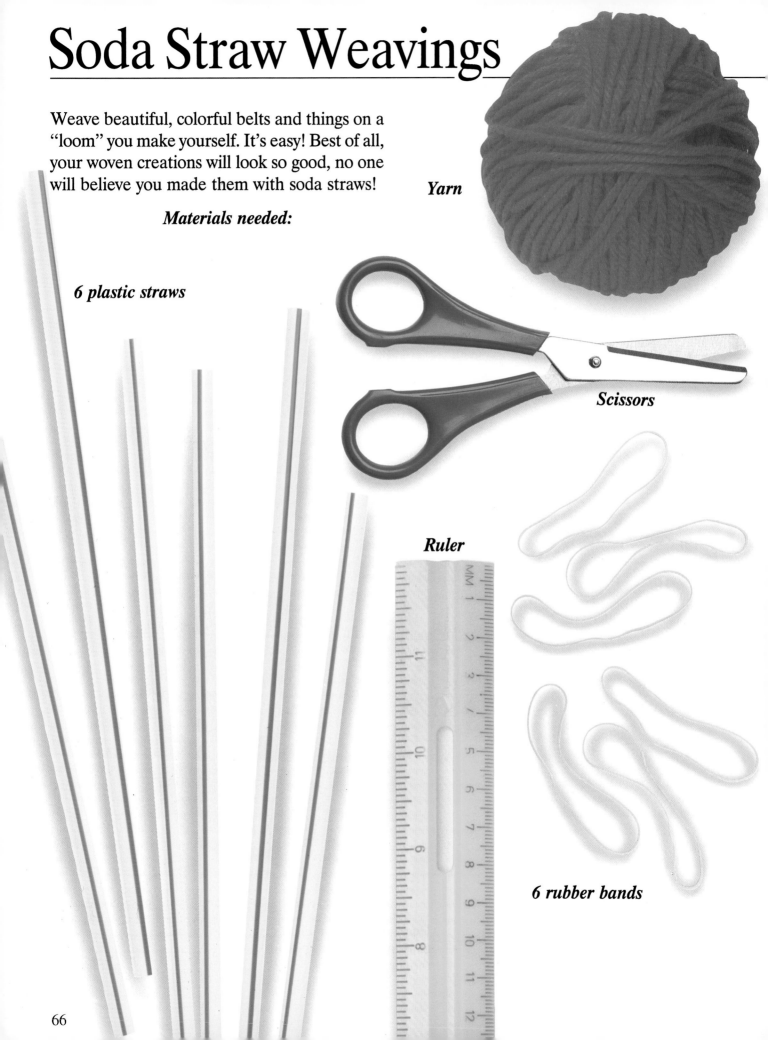

1 Cut six pieces of yarn 3' (1 m) long. These are called *warp* strings. Tie them together in a knot at one end—a starting knot.

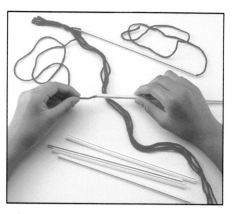

2 Push a plastic soda straw onto each warp string, right up to the starting knot.

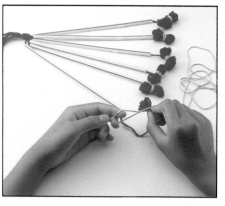

3 Wind the extra string hanging out of the end of each straw into a little ball and wrap it with a rubber band.

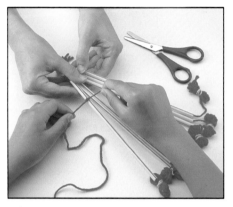

4 Cut another long piece of yarn—your *weaving* yarn. Tie one end onto one of the straws. Have someone help you hold the six straws in a row.

5 Start wrapping the weaving yarn over and under the straws. Weave around the last straw and back to where you started. Keep weaving back and forth.

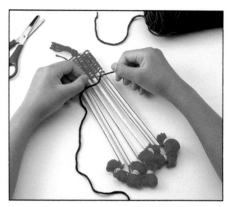

6 When you get near the end of the piece of weaving yarn, tie another long piece of yarn onto it and keep weaving. Change colors if you wish.

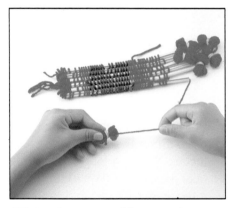

7 As the straws fill up, pull some of the yarn out of the balls at the ends of the warp strings.

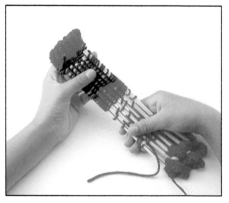

8 Push the woven part up onto the warp strings. Pull the straws down farther onto the yarn you pulled out of the balls. Then, weave some more.

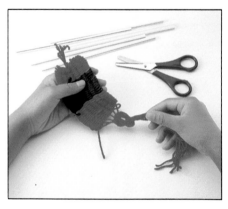

9 When you're finished weaving, tie the weaving yarn in a knot around one of the straws. Slip the straws off and tie an ending knot with all the warp strings.

Wearing Weavings

Ear Warmer
Tie a starting knot leaving 10″ of "tassle" hanging off the end of the knot. Weave until you have a strip long enough to fit over your head from ear to ear. Tie an ending knot leaving 10″ of tassle beyond the knot. Braid both tassles. Tie the braided ends behind your head under your hair.

Scarf
Dress up your doll or teddy bear! Start with warp strings as long as you want your scarf to be. Then weave the scarf and tie pretty tassles on each end.

Sash
Start with warp strings long enough to go around your waist plus several inches. Weave a long sash—it may take a couple of days to finish. Make a tassle at each end and tie the sash around your waist.

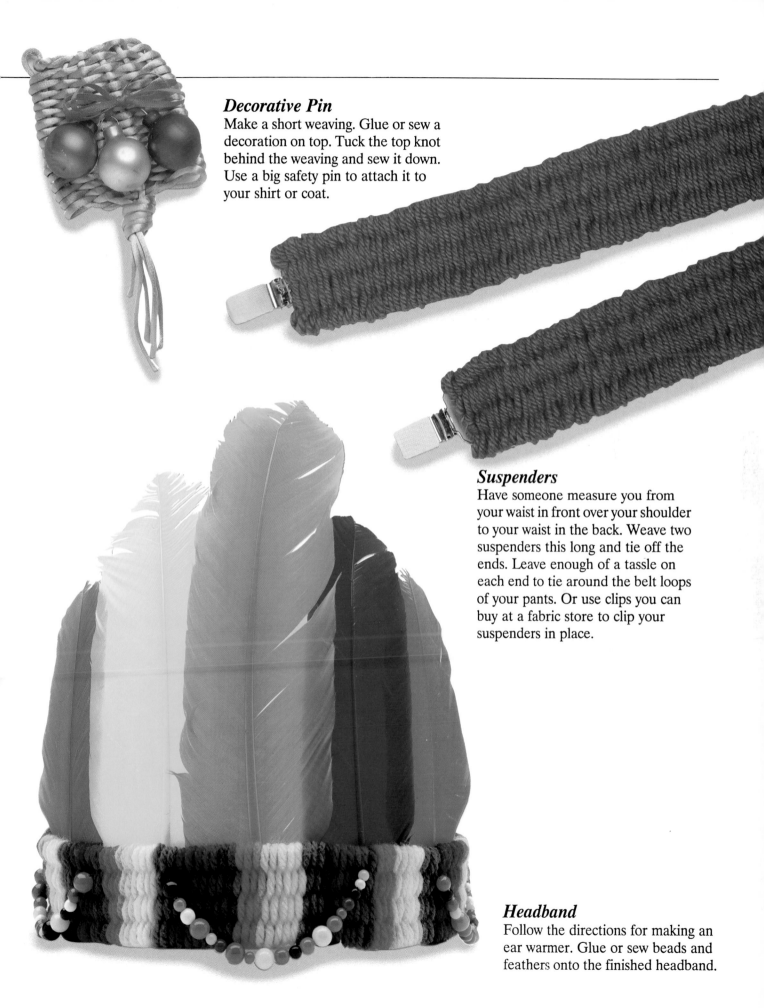

Decorative Pin
Make a short weaving. Glue or sew a decoration on top. Tuck the top knot behind the weaving and sew it down. Use a big safety pin to attach it to your shirt or coat.

Suspenders
Have someone measure you from your waist in front over your shoulder to your waist in the back. Weave two suspenders this long and tie off the ends. Leave enough of a tassle on each end to tie around the belt loops of your pants. Or use clips you can buy at a fabric store to clip your suspenders in place.

Headband
Follow the directions for making an ear warmer. Glue or sew beads and feathers onto the finished headband.

Critter Caps

Did you ever want to wear an alligator on your head? You can turn an old baseball hat into almost any animal. Start by choosing an animal to make. Look at pictures in wildlife books and magazines. You'll need to build the eyes, nose (or beak), ears, and horns if your animal has them. Use heavy paper, paper plates, or cardboard tubes. Decorate them with cut paper and fabric scraps. (You can buy the green foam for the alligator at craft stores.)

Once you put them together, you can't wash your critter caps. So wear them only on special days. When they wear out, pull the pieces off and use the hats to make new animals!

Materials needed:

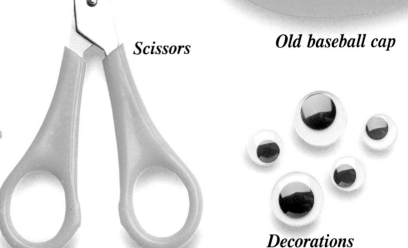

Scissors

Old baseball cap

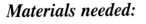

Glue

Decorations

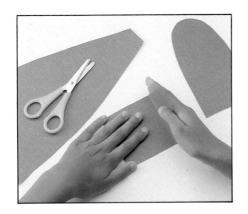

1 Cut a long triangle nose and two long rounded eye pieces out of heavy paper. Fold the rounded pieces in half so they'll stand up like the letter L.

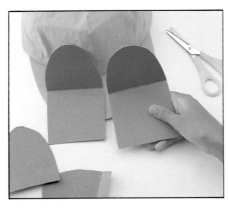

2 Hold the pieces up to the hat to see how they look. You may have to cut several test pieces until you get the size and shape you want.

3 Trace the paper pieces on the foam. Make the foam triangle bigger than the paper one. Cut the foam pieces out and glue them onto the paper.

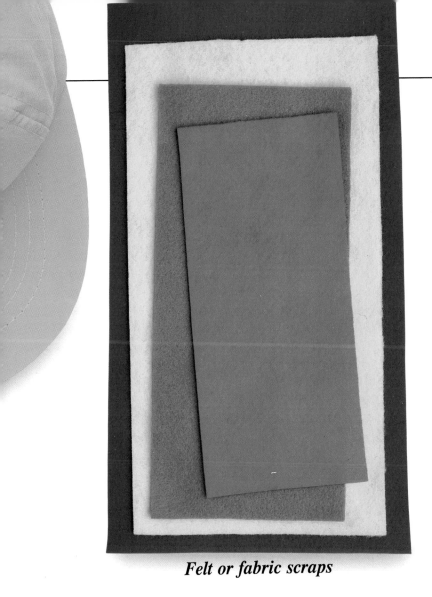

Felt or fabric scraps

Green foam

Felt pen

Light cardboard

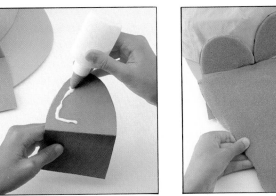

4 Glue the eyes onto the front of the cap so the bottom, flat part of the L lays on the cap's brim.

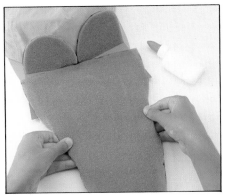

5 Glue the triangle nose onto the brim. Roll the sides of the foam under and glue them to the bottom of the paper to make a rounded lip.

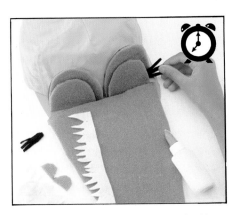

6 Add details: wiggly eyes, half-circle eyelids, felt teeth and eyelashes, half-circles of foam for nostrils, and anything else you think of. Let it dry overnight.

Critter Caps

Duck Cap

Dog Cap

Sheep Cap

Rabbit Cap

Alligator Cap

73

Towel Tops

Wear a work of art to the beach, pool, or any time you want to lounge around in style. Or, make an apron, tote bag or baby bib. After you sew your towel together, it's fun to stitch a picture on the front with colorful *embroidery*. If you've never sewn or embroidered before, ask an adult to help you.

Materials needed:

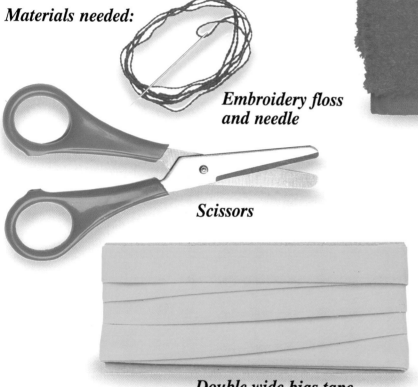

Embroidery floss and needle

Scissors

Double wide bias tape

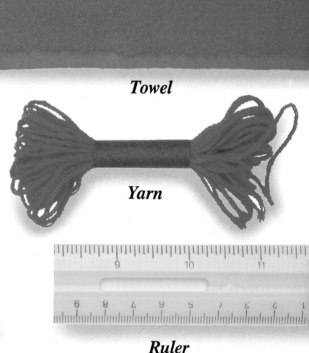

Towel

Yarn

Ruler

How to Sew

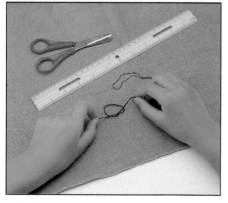

1 Cut a piece of thread about 24" (72 cm) long and poke it through the eye of a needle. Pull the ends even and tie a knot.

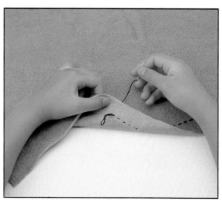

2 Sew with small stitches in and out of your fabric. Check each stitch to be sure your thread hasn't tangled underneath.

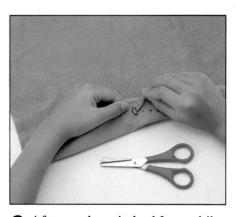

3 After you've stitched for a while, the thread will begin to get short. Push the needle to the back of your work, make a knot and cut the thread.

Make a Top

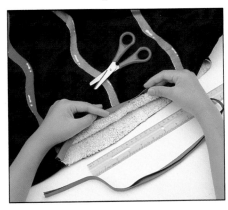

1 Fold your towel in half and cut a 9″ (27 cm) slit in the middle of the fold. Cut a 19″ (57 cm) piece of bias tape and cover the cut edge with it.

2 Cut off a long piece of embroidery floss and thread it through the needle. Make a knot at the end. Begin sewing, in and out, through the towel and bias tape.

3 Make a knot when you're done and cut off the extra floss. Sew up the sides of the towel the same way, leaving 12″ (36 cm) from the fold for arm holes.

Towel Tricks

You can make fancy borders on your Towel Tops by stitching along the edges. Make rows of chain stitches, or lines of different colored running stitches. Stitch a picture with cross-stitch. Plan your design on paper first. Then draw right on the towel with a pencil or chalk—the lines will wash out in the laundry.

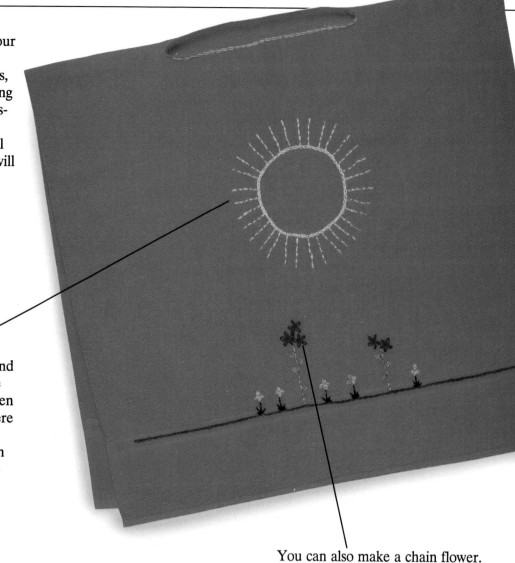

This sun was stitched with chain stitches and running stitches. To end a chain of chain stitches, bring the needle up inside your last loop. Then push it back into the cloth near where the needle came up, but on the *outside* of the loop. Make a knot in the back of the towel and trim the thread.

You can also make a chain flower. Make several chain stitches, going around in a circle, all starting at the same point.

Running Stitch

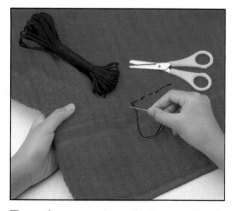

To make a running stitch, you simply sew in and out in a straight line. Be careful to make the stitches the same size and the same distance apart.

Cross-Stitch

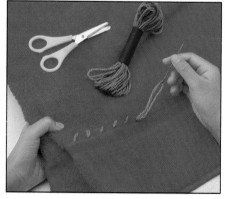

1 Cross-stitch uses little X shapes to color in big areas. Make a row of slanted lines going up from left to right.

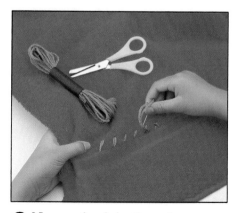

2 Now go back in the other direction, finishing each X by making a slanted line up from right to left.

76

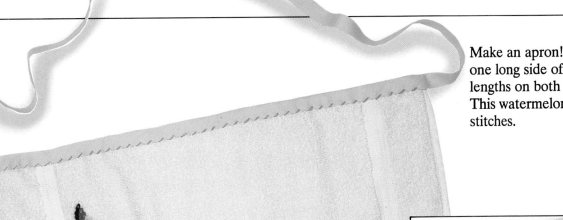

Make an apron! Sew bias tape along one long side of a towel leaving long lengths on both ends to be the ties. This watermelon is made of chain stitches.

Make a baby bib! Cut a half-circle for the neck and line it with bias tape, leaving long lengths on both ends to be the ties. This one is decorated with cross-stitches.

Chain Stitch

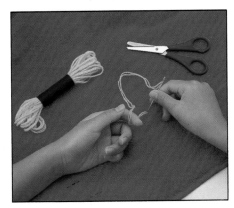

1 Bring the needle up from underneath the towel. Then push it back in, right next to where you came up.

2 Leave a loop of yarn setting on top of the towel. Bring the needle up from underneath again, inside the loop you just made!

3 Push the needle in right next to where you came up. Leave another loop setting on top of the towel. Make a long chain of loops.

Cloth Collage

Make beautiful pictures and abstract designs with cloth scraps, fabric glue and paint. Turn them into wall hangings or fun things to wear!

Materials needed:

Scissors

Fabric paint

Fabric scraps

Fabric glue

Decorations

1 Cut pieces of fabric to make an abstract pattern or a picture of a real thing. Arrange the pieces until you get a design you like.

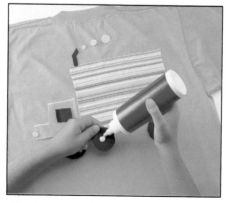

2 Lift the cut pieces one at a time, spread glue on the back, and set them in place. Glue the edges down well. Wash your hands often.

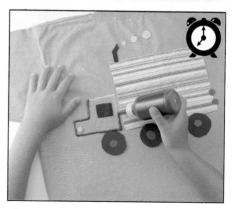

3 Outline the cut pieces with puffy fabric paint — it looks great, and holds them tight. Lay your finished collage flat to dry overnight.

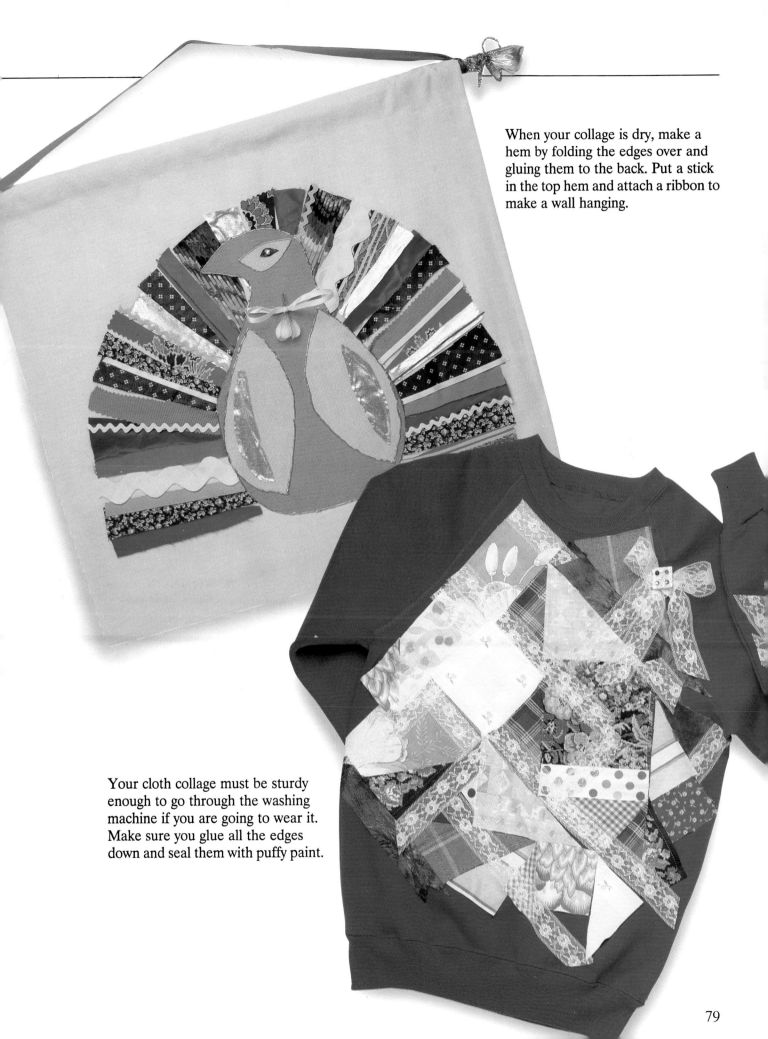

When your collage is dry, make a hem by folding the edges over and gluing them to the back. Put a stick in the top hem and attach a ribbon to make a wall hanging.

Your cloth collage must be sturdy enough to go through the washing machine if you are going to wear it. Make sure you glue all the edges down and seal them with puffy paint.

Jacket Jazz

Dress up your jackets with colorful decorations. Here are twelve things to try (from here to page 85). Read through all the directions before you begin—you may need special tools or supplies. Always plan your whole design and practice on scraps before you work on your good clothes.

Materials needed (in addition to a denim jacket):

Needle and thread

Fabric paint

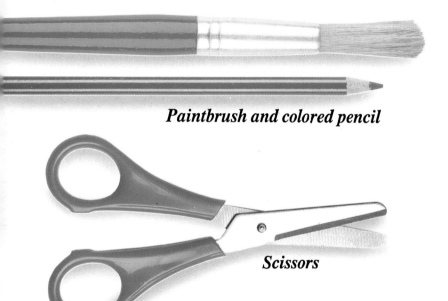

Paintbrush and colored pencil

Decorations

Scissors

Paper

Fabric glue

Star stencils and graffiti

Paint it. Draw a picture or pattern with a colored pencil, then color it in with fabric paint. Use lots of paint.

Graffiti. Draw block letters with a pencil, then fill in colors with fabric paint. Write your name, initials, or a funny saying.

Stencils. Cut a simple shape out of heavy paper. Trace it on your jacket with a colored pencil. Carefully color each one with fabric paint.

81

Jacket Fringe

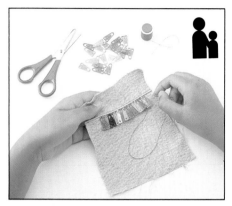

Bangles. Have an adult help you sew on plastic paperclips, charms, or buttons that hang down.

Beads. Put sparkly beads onto safety pins. Hook six or seven beaded pins together with one safety pin. Sew a row of these across your jacket.

1 **Fringe.** Cut strips of T-shirt material, felt or suede to fit under pocket flaps or along the bottom of the sleeves.

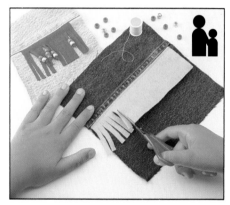

2 Have an adult help you sew on the cloth. Cut up into the cloth, but not all the way to the top. Tie on beads if you wish.

1 **Studs.** You can buy studs at fabric stores. There are kits to help you attach them (and jewels and coins!). Or, carefully poke them through the cloth by hand.

2 Turn the jacket over to the inside where the pointy ends of the studs poke through. Use a wooden spoon to bend them back against the fabric.

*Paper clip bangles
with painted centers*

*Studs and beaded
safety pins*

*Painted zebra pattern
and felt fringe*

83

Jacket Fluff

Ribbon and Lace. Attach ribbon, rickrack (zigzag cloth trim) and lace to your jacket with fabric glue. Follow the instructions on the fabric glue.

Glitter. Paint a picture or design on your jacket with fabric glue or fabric paint. Sprinkle glitter on it while the glue is wet. Let it dry overnight.

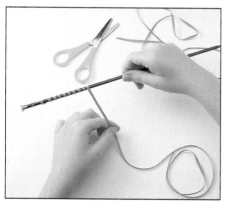

1 **Ribbon Curls.** Tightly wrap a metal knitting needle with cloth ribbon. Tie the ribbon around the needle at both ends. Soak it in water for a few minutes.

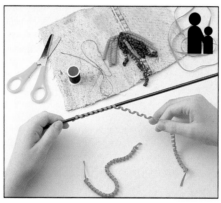

2 Have an adult help you "bake" it in a 250° F oven for an hour. When it's cool, unwind it and sew the curls to your jacket in bunches.

1 **Rag Puffs.** Use *pinking shears* to cut narrow strips of cloth. The shears make a zigzag edge that keeps the cloth from fraying.

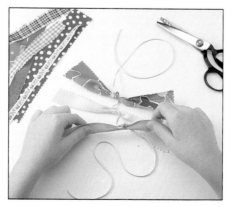

2 Cut the strips 7" (21 cm) long. Tie the strips in knots around a 9" (27 cm) piece of thin ribbon.

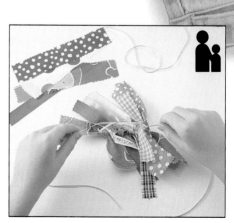

3 Tie the ribbon in a tight knot to gather the cloth strips into a puffy pompon. Have an adult help you sew the pompon to your jacket.

*Painted balloons
and ribbon curls*

Glitter and rickrack

Rag puffs

Tie-Dye T-Shirts

Tie a shirt up with string or rubber bands and dye it with fabric dye—*tie-dye!* Learn other methods using paper clips or a spray bottle. You can design lots of great shirts.

Be careful. The best place to tie-dye is outdoors on a warm day. If you work indoors, work over a sink and be very careful of drips and spills. Wear rubber gloves and old clothes.

Mixing fabric dyes: Buy dye at any supermarket. Have an adult help you mix a spoonful of dye with 2 cups of hot water in a bucket or glass jar.

Materials needed:

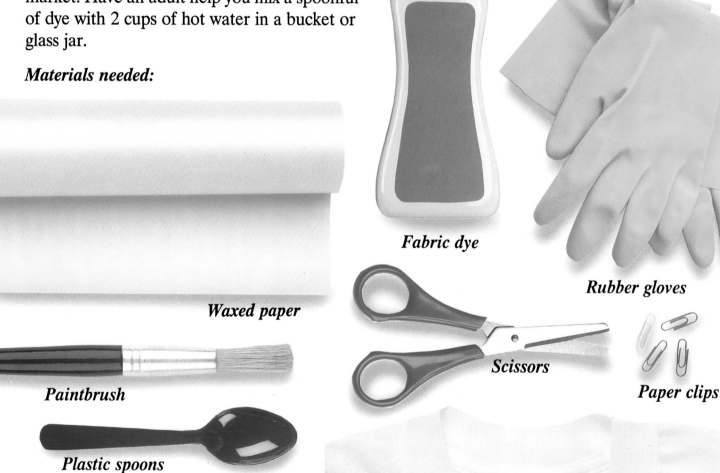

Bucket and hot water

Fabric dye

Rubber gloves

Waxed paper

Paintbrush

Scissors

Paper clips

Plastic spoons

T-shirt

String

Rubber bands

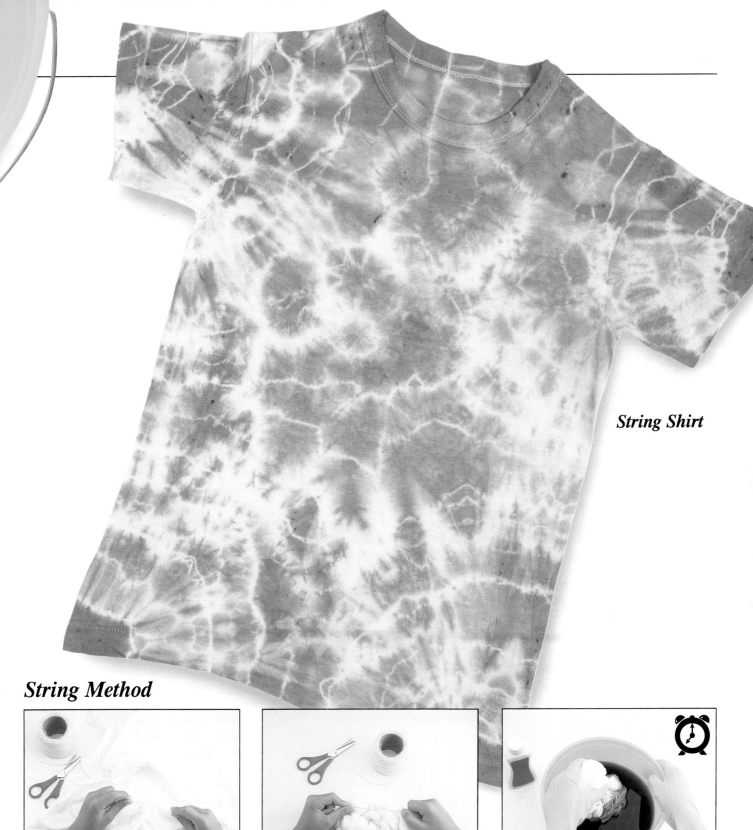

String Shirt

String Method

1 Tie a long piece of sturdy string onto a bottom corner of the T-shirt. Make it tight.

2 Crumple the shirt, wrapping the string *tightly* around the shirt as you crumple. Crumple and wrap the whole shirt and tie a knot.

3 Dip the shirt into dye for one minute. Let it set in the sink or out on the grass for a half hour before you undo the string.

87

Tie-Dye Tricks

Rubber Band Shirt

Rubber Band Method

Bull's-Eye
Poke up one big peak in the middle of the shirt. Wrap three rubber bands around it. Drip a different color into each section.

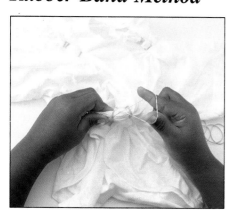

1 Poke up little peaks all over a T-shirt. Wrap each one with two rubber bands. Make them very tight.

2 Make three colors of dye. Use a spoon to carefully drip one color on the tip of each peak.

3 Drip a second color into the middle section of each peak. Drip a third color onto the body of the shirt. Let it set for a half hour. Undo the rubber bands.

Crumple a T-shirt into a long roll. Wrap string or rubber bands around the roll. Drip two colors of dye on it and let it set for a half hour.

Paper Clip Method

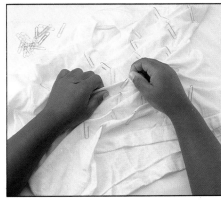

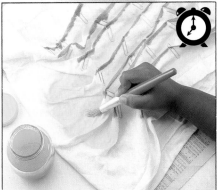

1 Lay a T-shirt flat and place sheets of waxed paper inside. Pinch up rows of folds across the front of the shirt. Use paper clips to hold them up.

2 Dip a paintbrush into dye and paint the top edges of the folds. Work slowly and let the dye soak into the cloth.

3 With a second color, paint a big sun in the corner and sunrays between the folds. Let the shirt dry completely before you take the waxed paper out.

Tie-Dye Pictures

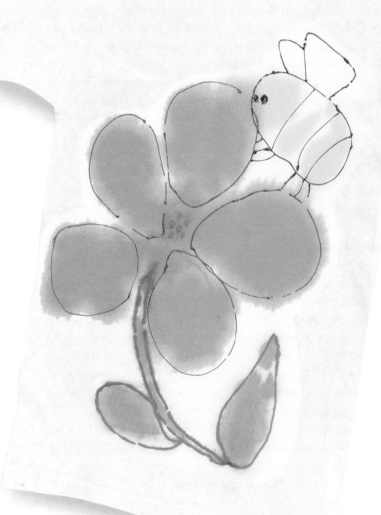

Freehand flower and bumble bee. Draw over your picture with fabric paints like puffy paint or glitter paint. They come in squeeze bottles so they're easy to draw with.

Freehand Method

1 Lay a T-shirt flat and put waxed paper inside. Make a big flower with a spoon or paintbrush. Work slowly—let the dye spread out.

2 Cut waxed paper shapes to cover your flower. Pour another color of dye into a spray bottle.

3 Put the shirt in a big box or outside on the grass. Spray dye on the T-shirt all around your flower. Let it dry completely.

Part Three: Make Cards!

A Note to Grown-Ups

Make Cards! features twenty-one projects that will result in quality cards kids will be proud to give or send. By inviting children to design their own cards, *Make Cards!* encourages individual creativity. Young artists will love doing these activities even while they're learning the importance of fine craftsmanship. Also, they'll be learning composition and design, working with color and texture, and planning symmetry versus abstract design. They'll even learn traditional bookbinding techniques.

Make Cards! develops not only artistic skills, but also fine motor skills and problem-solving abilities. Kids will decide to whom to send a card and for what occasion, plan the design, and then collect objects and supplies to create with. They'll engineer pop-up cards and construct edible candy cards. They'll plan peek-a-boo window cards. (What will be the surprise inside?) They'll invent board games and dot-to-dot puzzles, jigsaw puzzles and mazes. They'll make cards that will become three-dimensional boxes and pinwheels. They'll also learn easy ways to make wrapping paper and envelopes.

Getting the Most Out of the Projects

In *Make Cards!* kids learn by doing. They'll gain confidence as they experiment in various craft mediums. Giving handmade cards satisfies a kid's need for recognition of his or her work, something that giving store-bought cards can't do.

While the projects provide clear step-by-step instructions and photographs, each is open-ended so kids may decide what kind of cards *they* want to make. Most of the cards are shown without words on them so that kids can fill in their own ideas. In the text next to the cards, we've suggested things the cards *could* say, just to get kids started.

Collecting Supplies

In addition to the materials pictured on pages 92-93, you will need drawing paper; construction paper; cardboard; poster board; tracing paper; newspaper; black, sticky shelf paper; scissors; crayons; ruler; paint; glue; pencils; colored pencils and felt tip pens to complete these projects. Feel free to substitute! The projects offer flexibility to make it easy for you and your child to try as many activities as you wish.

Collecting Supplies

Here are some things you may use to make cards. You can probably find most of them around your home. If you have to buy some things, just remember that the cost of the supplies is part of the special gift— a card you made yourself!

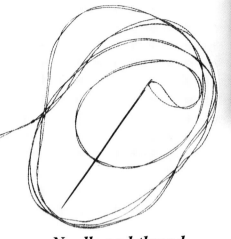

Needle and thread

Graham crackers

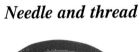

Nail

Masking tape

Electrical tape

String

Fabric scraps

Straw

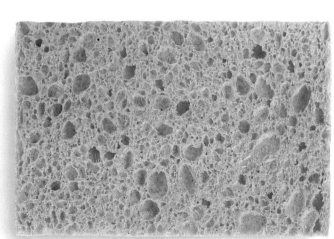

Sponge

Plastic wrap

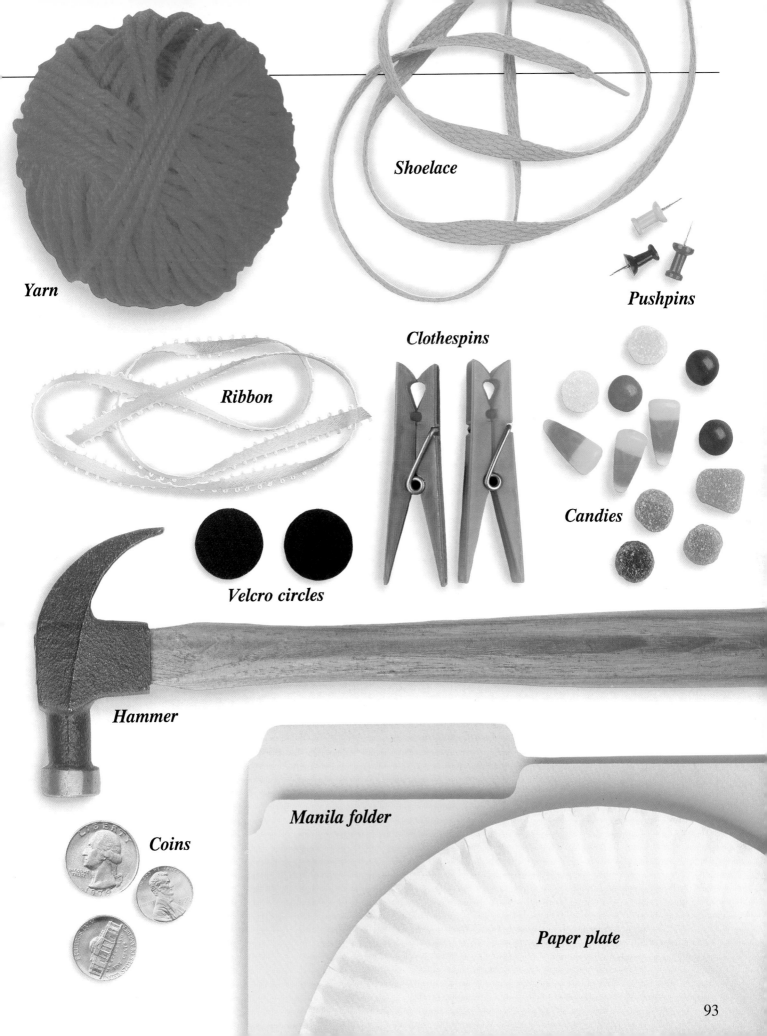

Yarn

Shoelace

Pushpins

Clothespins

Ribbon

Candies

Velcro circles

Hammer

Manila folder

Coins

Paper plate

93

Pull-Out Cards

There's more to these cards than meets the eye! They pull out and out and out to reveal a *long* message or picture.

Your card can pull out sideways or longways, whichever makes more sense for your picture. Glue a little tab on the back of the top panel for pulling.

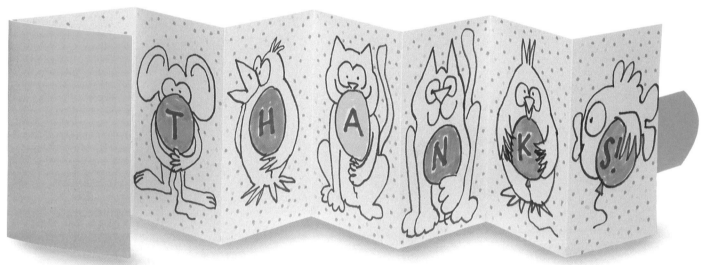

1 Make a cover for your card. Cut a piece of sturdy paper 6″ by 8″ (15 cm by 20 cm) and fold it in half. You can decorate the front of the cover if you wish.

2 Cut a strip of paper 6″ (15 cm) tall and 19″ (48 cm) long. Fold it like an accordion so each panel is about 3¾″ (9½ cm) wide.

3 Glue the folded paper to the inside of the card cover. Make sure the top accordion fold is on the *inside* next to the fold of the cover.

Painted flowers growing tall make a pretty Mother's Day card.

This card could say "Have a blast on your anniversary."

Shape Cards

These cute cards come in any shape you want:
hearts, sports cars, pigs, pizza or letters.
You trim the edges to fit your design.

A car-shaped card could say
"Wishing you a *speedy* recovery."

Do you have a special friend you
could send a card to—in the shape of
his or her own name?

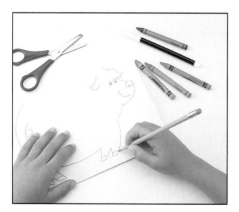

1 Fold a piece of paper in half to make a card. The fold can be at the top or the side of the card. Make a drawing with one edge touching the fold.

2 Color your picture with crayons, paint or felt-tip pens. Draw a smooth, solid line all around the drawing if you wish.

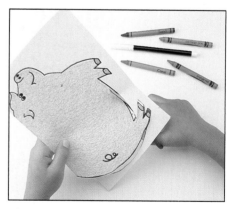

3 Cut along the outside line, through both layers of paper. *Don't* cut along the fold! Open your shape, color the inside, and write a message.

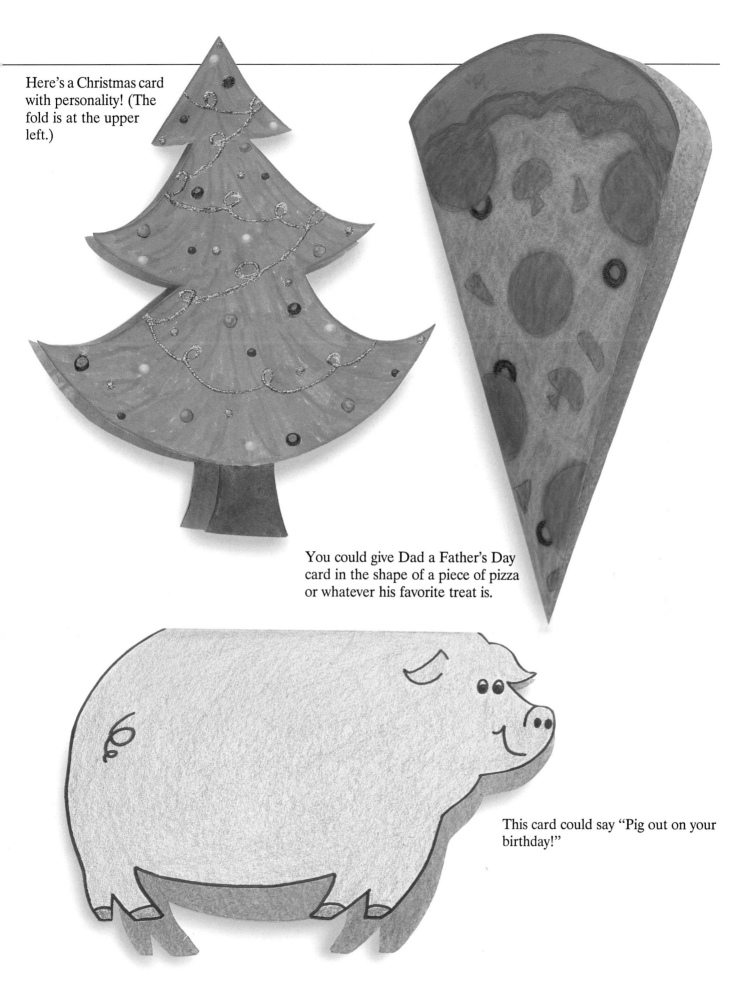

Here's a Christmas card with personality! (The fold is at the upper left.)

You could give Dad a Father's Day card in the shape of a piece of pizza or whatever his favorite treat is.

This card could say "Pig out on your birthday!"

Window Cards

These cards are sure to make someone smile. Cut a "window" in the front cover. Paste a photo or draw a picture on the inside. Only part of the picture shows through. When you open the card—surprise!

This house card could say "Congratulations on your new home."

A camera card.

This fence card could say "Have some good, clean fun this Grandparent's Day!"

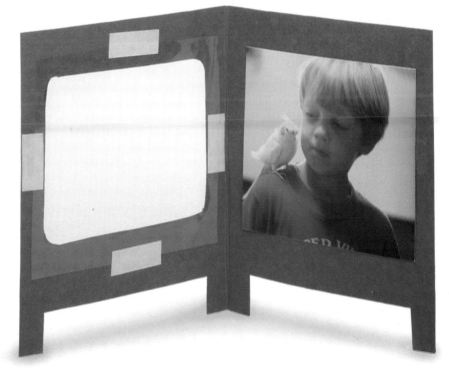

A TV card could say "You're the star of the show!" Tape plastic wrap behind the window and it will look like a shiny TV screen.

Toy Cards

When is a card not just a card? When it's a toy! Send your friends something really special: a card they can play with. Send the pinwheel or snake flat, with directions for how to make them work.

Silly Snake

Send the snake to someone as a flat card, shown above. Tell him or her to cut out the snake by cutting all the way up the spiral line and around the head.

When the snake is cut out, it will hang in a spiral as you can see to the right. Blow on it, and it will do a twisting dance!

Pinwheel

This pinwheel has two different sides. Before it's put together, it's just a flat square, shown at the top of the page. Send it to someone with a pushpin, a brand new pencil, and the directions (on the next page).

To the left you can see what the pinwheel looks like all folded up and ready to spin! Turn it around with your hands until it moves easily. Then blow on it for a really fast spin!

Pinwheel Card

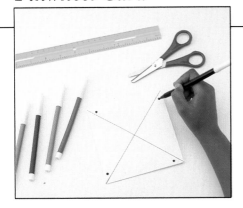

1 Cut a piece of heavy paper into a square that's 5″ (13 cm) on each side. Draw an "X." Make four dots, as shown.

2 Cut each line 2½″ (6½ cm) in from the corners. *Don't* cut all the way to the middle! Poke a hole in the center with a nail or pushpin.

3 Decorate both sides of the pinwheel. This one says, "You're a nice friend" on one side, and has a colorful design on the back.

Pinwheel Directions

1 Here are directions to send with your card: Push the pushpin up through one of the corner dots. Bend the paper in so the pin is over the center hole.

2 One by one, bend each paper corner under the pushpin and push up. Push all the other dots up onto the pin. Be careful not to poke your finger.

3 When all the corners are on the pushpin, push it through the center hole of the pinwheel. Poke it straight into the eraser of the pencil.

Silly Snake Card

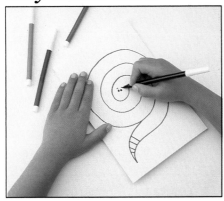

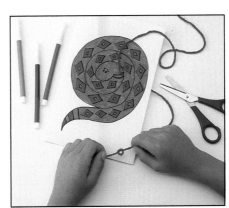

1 On the front of a folded card, draw a long snake all coiled up.

2 Decorate the snake with bold markings.

3 Color both sides of the snake. Poke a hole at the head of the snake. Tie on a long piece of yarn.

Game Cards

Game cards make good Get Well cards. On the front cover you could write "Hope you're feeling better soon. Here's a little something to cheer you."

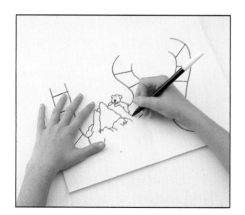

1 Fold a card out of strong paper 9″ by 12″ (size A4). On the inside, draw a path and divide it into spaces. Make barriers or shortcuts.

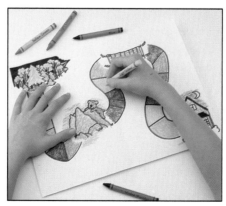

2 Draw a color in each space or write directions like, "Jump ahead 3 spaces." Draw pictures around the path.

3 You can write instructions around the border of your game. Or make up cards to show players which space to move to.

IF YOU LAND ON AN ARROW, GO INTO THE SIDE
PATH. IF YOU LAND ON A MESSAGE, FOLLOW IT. IF
YOU LAND ON ANOTHER PLAYER, THEY GO
BACK 4 SPACES. FIRST ONE TO THE FINISH WINS!
START
GO BACK TO START
GO BACK 2
MISS ONE TURN
JUMP AHEAD 4
SWITCH WITH LEADER
MISS 2 TURNS
TAKE AN EXTRA TURN
GO BACK FOUR
GO BACK TO THE STAR
SKIP YOUR NEXT TURN
FINISH

A finished board game.

-2

You can buy dice and game pieces if you wish. Or, make cards to show where the players should move and use buttons or coins for game pieces.

Book Cards

Most cards are made up of just one piece of paper folded into two pages. But you can make a card that is a whole book of pages! The more pages you put in, the more it will look like a real book. Make a little joke book and write one of your favorite jokes or riddles on each page. Tie it with a shoelace for an extra laugh. Or make a book to fill with your special family photos.

A photo album. If you like how the stitches look, you don't *have* to cover them with tape.

A book of jokes and riddles.

1 Measure and cut two pieces of poster board for the book covers. Make lots of pages out of heavy paper or poster board. Cut them all the same size.

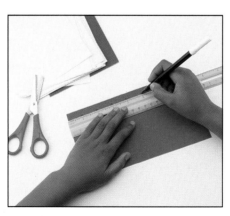

2 Use a ruler and make a line of dots along one edge of one of the covers. Make the marks 1″ (2½ cm) apart.

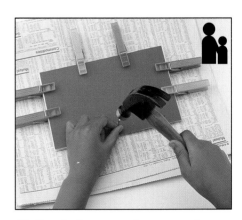

3 Stack the pages between the covers (put the marked cover on top). Hold it with clothespins. Set it on a stack of newspaper. Carefully nail a hole at each mark.

A picture book is the perfect card to say "Welcome, new baby." The cover looks like a building block. The inside pages are filled with big, colorful pictures for the baby to look at.

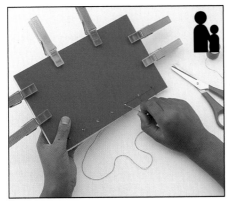

4 Cut a long piece of thread. Poke it through the hole of a needle. Bring the ends together and tie a knot. Make lots of stitches through the nail holes.

5 Wrap a strip of colored electrical tape or glue-covered paper around the edge of the book that is stitched.

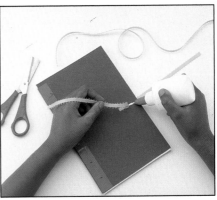

6 Glue a short piece of ribbon on the front and back covers. When the glue is dry, tie the book closed!

Book Cards

This house-shaped card is a family scrapbook. It is held together with *brads* (little, bendable metal clips). Each page has drawings and stuff collected from someone in the family.

▲ Here's the outside of the scrapbook.

Here's the inside of the scrapbook.

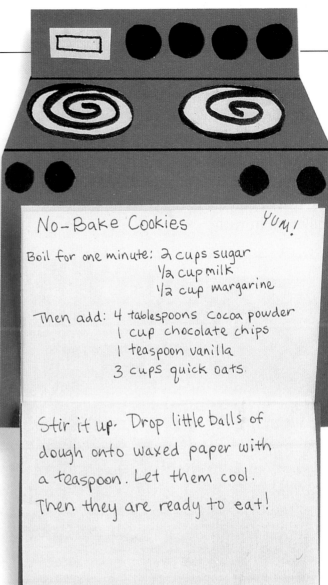

No-Bake Cookies YUM!

Boil for one minute: 2 cups sugar
½ cup milk
½ cup margarine

Then add: 4 tablespoons cocoa powder
1 cup chocolate chips
1 teaspoon vanilla
3 cups quick oats.

Stir it up. Drop little balls of
dough onto waxed paper with
a teaspoon. Let them cool.
Then they are ready to eat!

Make an oven-shaped card! This one
is stapled instead of stitched. The
oven door opens to reveal all your
favorite recipes. A great card for
someone who loves to cook or bake.

A note pad "book card" is a very
useful gift!

Collage Cards

Piece by piece, bits of paper and scraps of cloth may not look like much. But put them all together and you can make beautiful *collage* cards. A collage is a picture made up of pieces of cut paper or other little things. Half the fun of collage cards is looking for stuff to make them with!

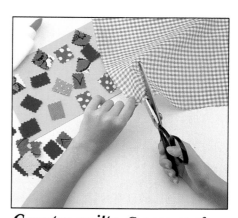

Paper collages are fun and easy to put together for any holiday or special occasion.

This robot looks like he's running away from a robot dog. He'd be a cheerful card for someone who is ill. The inside could say "Hope you're on your feet again soon!"

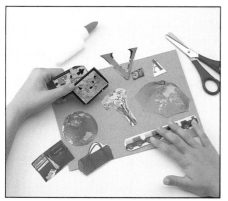

Paper collage. Cut pictures and letters out of old magazines. Arrange these pieces on the front of a folded card. Glue or tape them in place.

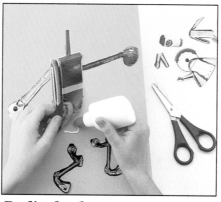

Radical robots. Look through magazines and catalogs for pictures of machines and metal things. Carefully cut them out and glue them together to make robots.

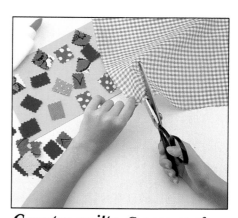

Country quilts. Cut scraps of cloth into little squares. Glue them on the front of a folded card. Draw stitches around each square.

Quilt collage cards can say "I'm glad we're friends," or any message you want to send. Cutting with *pinking shears* makes the cloth edges zigzagged.

This rainbow really looks like a *mosaic* made of colored tiles. Glue or tape your finished mosaic onto the front of a folded card.

Tile Mosaic Card

1 Cut a piece of black, sticky, shelf paper. Place it sticky-side-up on a piece of cardboard. Hold the edges down with masking tape.

2 Cut little shapes out of colored paper. Stick them on the black paper to make an abstract design or a picture. Leave a little black between the shapes.

3 Cut a piece of clear, sticky, shelf paper to fit over your mosaic. Carefully put it sticky-side-down. Smooth it and trim the edges. Cut the masking tape off, too.

Collage Cards

A candy collage makes a sweet treat for any special day.

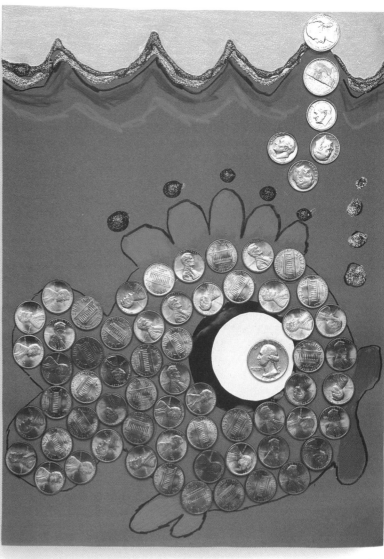

A coin collage would make a great "Good luck" card.

Candy Card

1 You will need small candies like candy corn and chocolate bits. Arrange them on a graham cracker so they make a picture.

2 Make frosting "glue" by stirring a teaspoon of milk or water into ¼ cup of powdered sugar.

3 One at a time, lift the candies off the cracker. Dip just the bottoms into frosting. Set them back in place. Let it dry overnight.

Straw collage card

A collage of lace, flowers, hearts and cupids makes a beautiful valentine.

Straw Card

1 Cut a cardboard rectangle. Paint it black—acrylic paint is best. Let the paint dry.

2 Cut the straw into strips. Glue these onto the black board to create a picture. When you're done, let the glue dry completely.

3 Brush acrylic varnish over the finished picture. When it's dry, glue it onto the front of a folded card a little bigger than the board.

Print Cards

Dip a cookie cutter in paint and stamp it to make a print. Or, cut wild shapes out of foam or sponges to print with. It's so much fun, you'll want to make lots of these easy print cards. You can also make wrapping paper to match!

Print cards are fun and easy to make just to say "Thinking of you," "I miss you," or "Please write."

A heart-shaped friendship card.

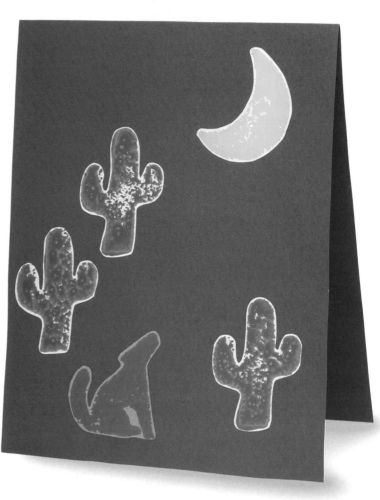

Sponge Stamps

1 You can buy little sponge shapes to make prints with. Or, cut your own simple shapes out of sponges or foam.

2 Spread a thin layer of tempera paint on a plate. Press a sponge shape into the paint. Then stamp it onto paper to make a print.

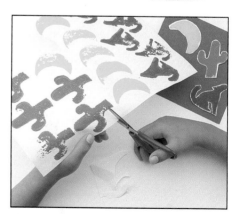

3 Make lots of prints. Pick the best ones, cut them out, and glue them onto your card.

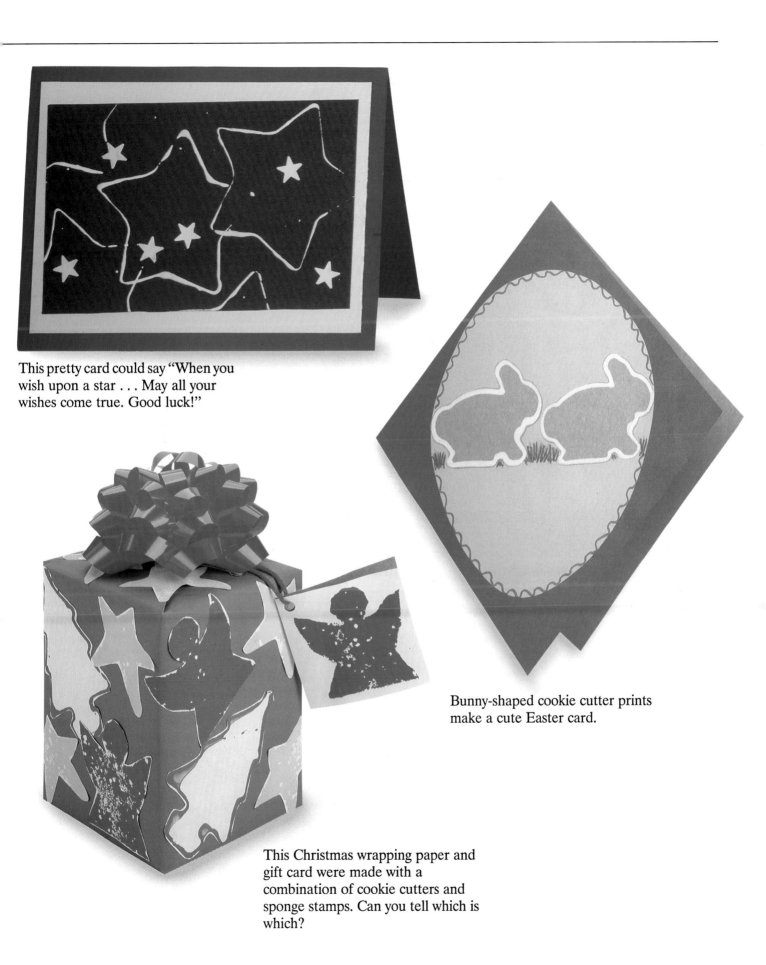

This pretty card could say "When you wish upon a star . . . May all your wishes come true. Good luck!"

Bunny-shaped cookie cutter prints make a cute Easter card.

This Christmas wrapping paper and gift card were made with a combination of cookie cutters and sponge stamps. Can you tell which is which?

Trickster Cards

Here are some tricky cards your friends and relatives will love to open. After you try these four ideas, make up your own special trickster cards!

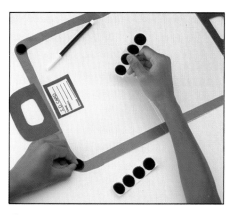

A briefcase card makes a perfect birthday card for a hardworking dad or mom.

Briefcase Card

1 Draw a briefcase on a manila folder with the bottom edge on the fold. Color your drawing or use cut paper to make your card look like a real briefcase.

2 Cut out the briefcase shape. Decorate the inside of the card to look like the inside of a briefcase. Put velcro circles in the top corners to hold it closed.

3 Cut strips of paper to make pockets and glue them inside the briefcase. Make little paper pens, a note pad and a calculator.

This box is made of two layers of paper glued together. A manila folder makes it strong. Brown paper makes it look like a real mailing package.

Box Card

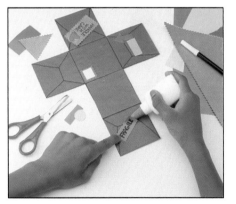

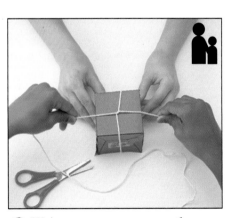

1 On a piece of sturdy paper 9″ by 12″ (size A4), draw a 3″ (7 cm) square. Then draw five more squares the same size to make a cross shape.

2 Cut out the cross shape. Fold at each line you drew to make six squares. Open it up and decorate the outside to look like a package.

3 Write your message on the inside. Fold the box and tie it closed with a piece of string. (It's easier to tie if someone holds it closed for you.)

Trickster Cards

A shoe makes a funny *belated* (a late) birthday card. On the inside, write, "I could kick myself for forgetting your birthday. Hope it was happy!"

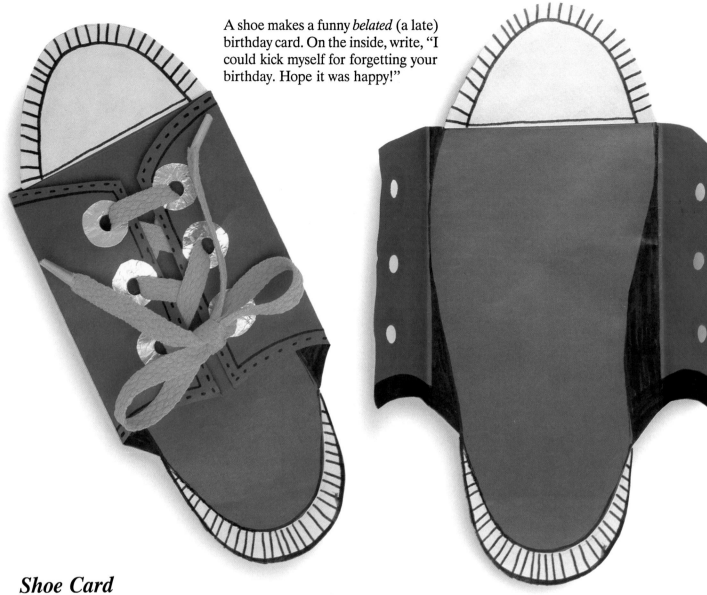

Shoe Card

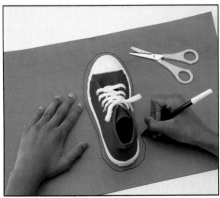

1 Put a shoe in the middle of a big piece of sturdy paper and trace around it. Use the shoe as a guide when you color your card.

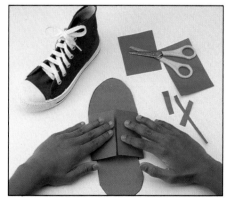

2 Draw flaps on both sides of the shoe. Cut out the shoe and flaps as one big piece. Make the flaps big at first, then fold them in and trim them until they meet in the middle.

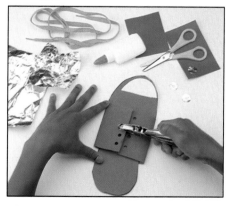

3 Make holes in the flaps for the laces. A hole punch works best. Write a message under the flaps and decorate the shoe with colored paper and foil.

116

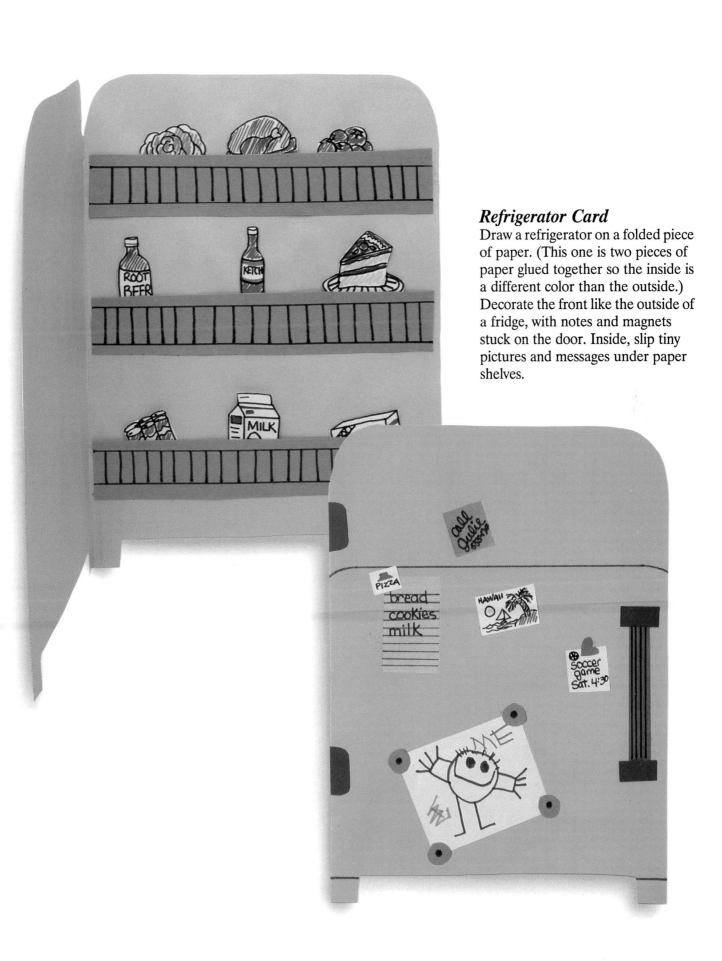

Refrigerator Card

Draw a refrigerator on a folded piece of paper. (This one is two pieces of paper glued together so the inside is a different color than the outside.) Decorate the front like the outside of a fridge, with notes and magnets stuck on the door. Inside, slip tiny pictures and messages under paper shelves.

Yarn Cards

These cards are soft, fuzzy and fun to touch.
You make the designs with pieces of brightly
colored yarn.

*Finished
Flower Card*

Gift Card

Flower Card

1 Draw a simple picture on the
front of a folded card. Cut long
pieces of yarn in the colors you want
for your picture.

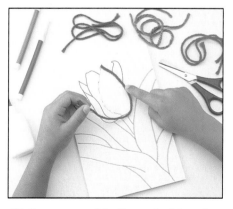

2 Squeeze a thin line of white glue
along the lines you drew. Gently
lay the yarn along the glue lines.
Push the yarn down into the glue as
you go.

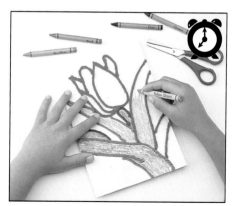

3 Cover all the lines in your
drawing with yarn. Let the glue
dry. Then color the paper behind
your yarn drawing with felt pens or
crayons.

Good Luck Card
This rainbow was painted with watercolor paints. Then yarn was added between the stripes of color.

Note Card
This duck was made like the flower card, but yarn was used instead of crayons to color in all the shapes.

Hi, Grandma! Hi, Grandpa!

Use a hole punch or scissors to make holes around the front cover of a card. Then weave yarn in and out to make a frame for a cute photograph. It's easier to weave if you wrap tape around the tip of the yarn.

We've Moved

Cut a scrap of checkered material. Stitch X's in the checks to make a picture. Glue the picture onto the front of a card!

Great Ball o' Yarn

Collect little toys and candies. Tie them onto a *long* piece of yarn as you wind it into a big ball. Keep wrapping until all the toys and candies are hidden inside the ball of yarn. When your friend unwinds the ball of yarn, she'll discover one surprise after another!

Personalized Birthday Card

Cover the front of a card with sticky shelf paper that looks like wood. Use string or twine to write a name. The "I" in this card was dotted with a metal "spur" for a real Western look.

Wedding Card

Cut a small piece of mesh from a bag of apples or oranges. Cut a hole into the front of a card. Tape the mesh on the *inside* of the front of the card, covering the hole. Weave yarn into the mesh and decorate the front of the card.

Pop-Up Cards

These fancy cards really stand up to the occasion! Open them—and a silly face, birthday cake, spaceship, or vase of flowers pops to life. You build the 3-D designs with special folds and paper hinges.

Here's the cover of a face pop-up card.

Here's the inside of the face pop-up card—going bonkers!

1 Cut and fold a sturdy piece of paper to make a card cover.

2 Cut out the pieces you need for your picture. On this person, the shirt and head are flat against the inside of the card, so they are glued down first.

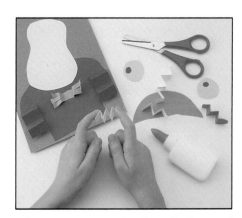

3 Make paper "springs." Cut three thin strips of paper. Fold them into zigzags. On this person, the bow tie and arms were folded into zigzags, too.

This festive cake pops up for a very Happy Birthday card.

This card could say "Your gift was out of this world! Thank you!"

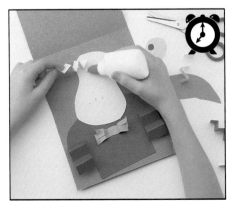

4 Glue one end of each spring onto the card where you want something to pop up. Let the glue dry before going on.

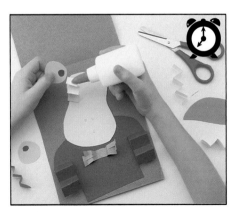

5 Glue the other end of each spring to the back of a pop-up piece. Let the glue dry. When you close the card, gently fold the springs closed.

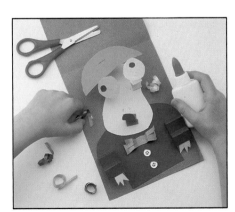

6 Add decorations. This person has swirls for nostrils, a zigzag tongue, hands, buttons and ribbons.

Pop-Up Cards

Here's the finished flower vase card. Be careful when you close this card—don't smash the flowers! Send it to someone to say "Thank you," "Get well," "Congratulations," or for any occasion when you might send flowers.

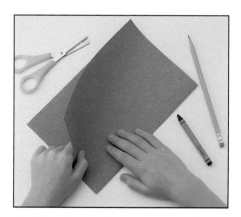

1 Here's another way to make a pop-up card. Start by making a sturdy paper cover.

2 For a flower vase card, cut flowers and stems out of colorful construction paper.

3 Cut a paper vase. It should be a little smaller than half the size of your card. Fold it in half. Fold each edge back to make two flaps.

You can make a "sideways" pop-up card. The "V"-shaped fold makes a park bench for kids and animals to sit on! This card could say "Happy Birthday" or "You are special."

4 Open the card cover. Hold the vase over the center fold. Hold it so the "V" shape stands up a little. Mark one of the flap edges.

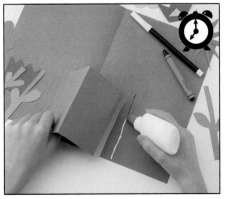

5 Spread glue along the line and set the flap down in place. Glue the other flap to the other side of the cover. Let it dry.

6 Glue some of the flowers to the card cover. Glue some to the inside of the vase so they pop up. Add sequins and cut paper shapes.

Puzzle Cards

Give your friends and family something to think about with these mysterious puzzle cards. Make a jigsaw puzzle or hidden message card — they'll have to solve the puzzle to get your message. Or design a dot-to-dot puzzle or a maze just for fun. You can make them easy to do or hard to do — it's up to you!

Here's how your jigsaw puzzle card will look when it's cut into pieces.

Here's another puzzle card before it's cut apart. You could send it to someone just to celebrate the first day of summer (June 21).

Jigsaw Puzzle

1 Draw a picture on a piece of heavy paper. Color your picture with crayons, colored pencils or felt-tip pens. Write a message in big letters on the back.

2 Divide your picture into puzzle pieces. Draw twisty lines in black. Make all the pieces about the same size — and not too small.

3 Cut the pieces apart and put them in an envelope. The person who gets this card will have to put the puzzle together to read the message on the back.

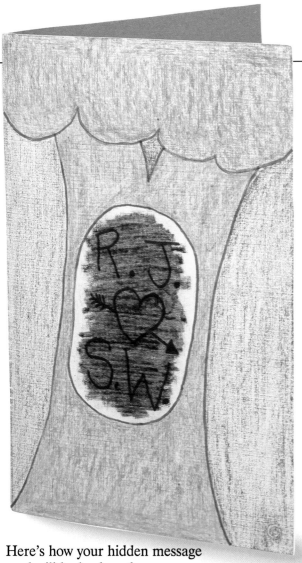

Here's how your hidden message card will look when the person scratches off the black. Use the entire inside of the card to write a love letter!

Another way to send a secret message is to write on white paper with a white crayon. The special instructions would say "To read this card, paint it with watercolors!"

Hidden Message

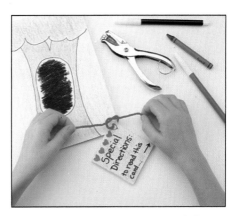

1 Write a message on a card, by itself or inside a drawing. This card is made to look like initials carved into a tree.

2 Color over the whole message with black crayon. Make it dark so the message doesn't show through the black.

3 With this card, send special instructions that say: "To read this card, use a coin to scratch off the black crayon."

127

Puzzle Cards

Dot-to-Dot

 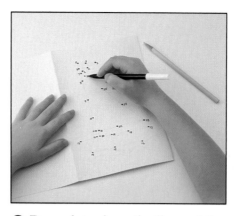 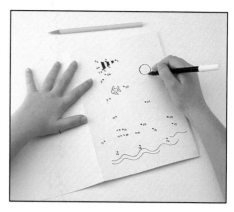

1 Fold a piece of paper in half. Draw a simple picture on one half. Fold another piece and lay it on top. This top paper will be the card.

2 Draw dots along the lines of the main thing in your drawing. Make a dot wherever the lines change direction. Number the dots.

3 Draw the details that are not part of the dot-to-dot drawing. Make a colorful border around the card, if you wish.

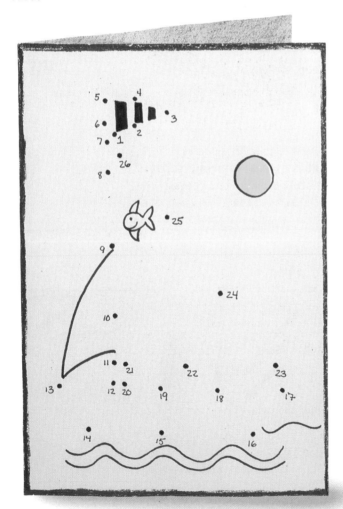

Here's how your finished dot-to-dot card will look when your friend gets it.

Here's how your puzzle will look after your friend has filled it in! Inside, it could say "Have a great vacation!"

Maze

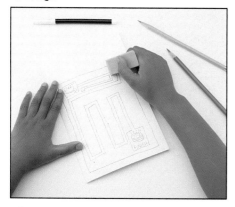

1 Draw a simple path. Then start to make dead-end paths (shown here in red). Erase the main path where the dead-ends begin.

2 Add more dead-end paths until you can hardly tell what the real path is! The more dead-ends you add, the harder it will be to solve.

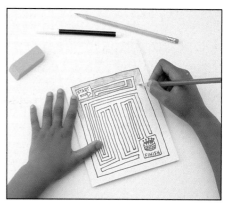

3 Go over all the lines of your puzzle with a black felt-tip pen. Be careful to cover the lines completely. Color in the background.

Come to my Birthday Party!

START →

FINISH

Here's how a maze can become an invitation. On a photocopy machine, you can make lots of copies on colored paper. Use crayons to add extra color. On the inside, write:

Who: _____ (your name)

What: <u>A Birthday Party!</u>

Where: _____ (your address)

When: _____ (the date and time of the party)

RSVP: _____ (your phone number —this means people should call and tell you if they can come). Make envelopes to send them in. See pages 130-131 for envelope instructions.

Envelopes

Make beautiful envelopes to fit all of your special cards. Use writing paper, colored construction paper, or the inside of a paper grocery bag! If you are going to mail your envelope, use shelf paper (from a supermarket). It's light and sturdy, and it won't get hurt if it gets wet.

▲ This looks like an envelope. It's really a letter folded in thirds and held together with a sticker.

◀ Finished basic envelope from the back.

Basic Envelope

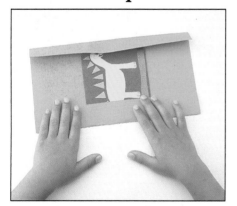

1 Lay your card in the middle of a big piece of paper. Fold the two sides of the paper in over the card.

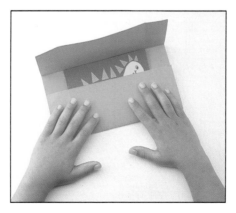

2 Fold the bottom edge up over the card and the top edge down. The card should fit perfectly inside the folds.

3 Open the folds and cut out the corner rectangles.

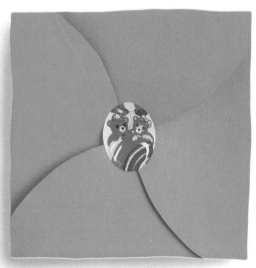

Make a fancy envelope for a square card. Cut four flaps like flower petals. Fold them over the card one at a time. Hold them together with a sticker.

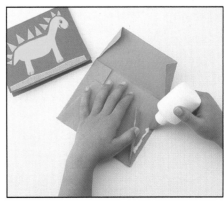

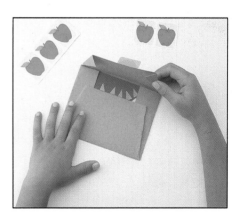

4 Fold slanted flaps on the top and bottom parts of the envelope.

5 Fold the sides of the envelope in. Fold the bottom up and glue the flaps to the sides of the envelope.

6 Slip the card inside and fold the top of the envelope down over it. Glue it down or hold it with a sticker.

Here's a fold-a-note shown closed and open. Cut a long piece of paper with a point at the top. Write a letter on one side. Fold it in thirds, with the letter on the inside. Hold it closed with a sticker.

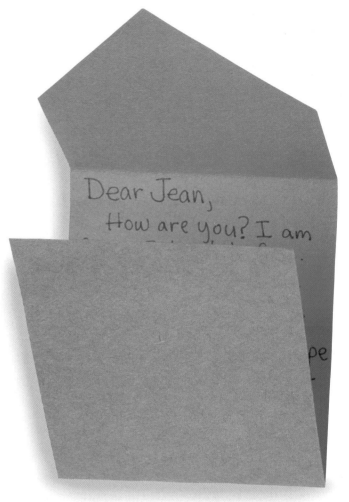

Make handmade or store-bought envelopes more fun with envelope art! If you draw on the front, leave a space for the name and address.

Part Four: Make Gifts!

A Note to Grown-Ups

Make Gifts! features eleven unique projects that invite children to design their own gifts. Young artists will love doing these activites even while they're learning the importance of fine craftsmanship. And they'll be learning composition and design, working with color and texture, and planning symmetry versus abstract design.

Make Gifts! involves not only artistic skills, but also fine motor skills and problem solving. Kids will engineer pop-up cards and plan functional calendars. They'll get a workout pounding hardware into wood. They'll create gift bundles that smell good. They'll gain experience in many different craft media. Giving crafted gifts satisfies kids' need for recognition of their work, something not achievable with store-bought gifts.

Collecting Supplies

All of the projects can be done with household items or inexpensive, easy-to-find supplies. Here are some household items you'll want to make sure you have on hand: empty cans, bottles and jars; scrap paper and scrap cloth; sponges; metal pieces and hardware; newspapers; paper plates; masking tape and duct tape; string, ribbon and yarn; foam trays; sandpaper; paper towels; a muffin tin; an old toothbrush.

Trophies

Trophies are for winners, and anyone who gets one of these handmade awards is a winner for sure! Each trophy is a sculpture—a one-of-a-kind character you design yourself. It's fun to build trophies using materials related to whatever the award is. Here are instructions for making The World's Greatest Cook trophy. Look on pages 136-137 for more ideas—or make up your own!

Materials needed:

White glue

Plastic measuring cup

Macaroni

Scissors

Things to make a face

1 Glue macaroni onto the measuring cup head to make a wild hairdo. Work slowly, letting the glue dry as you work.

2 Draw a smiling face with a felt-tip pen, or glue on raisins or other small things a cook would use. Let this dry overnight.

3 Cover the empty can with construction paper. Carefully cut small slits into two sides. Stick the plastic spoons in for the arms.

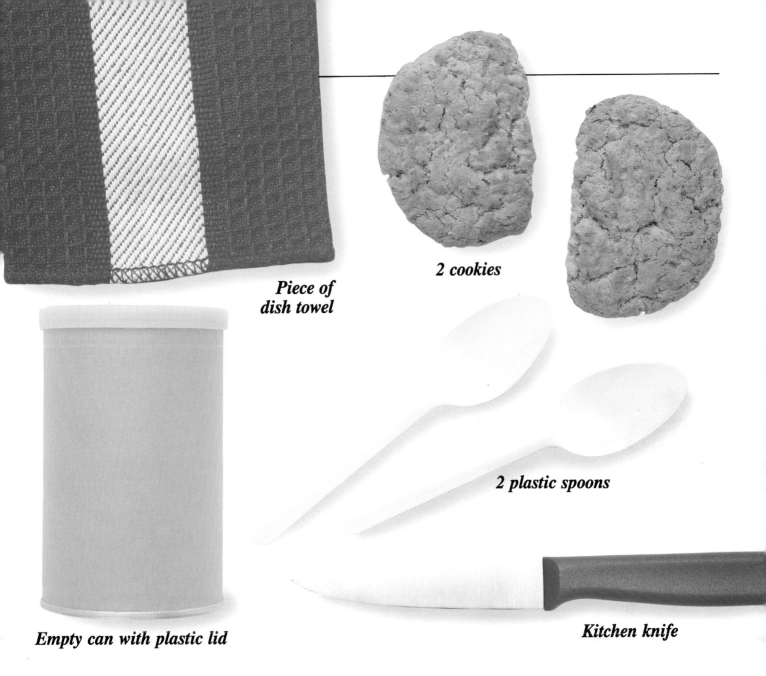

Piece of dish towel

2 cookies

2 plastic spoons

Empty can with plastic lid

Kitchen knife

4 Glue the cookies onto the bottom of the can for big, sturdy feet. Cut a slit into the plastic lid and slip in the measuring cup head.

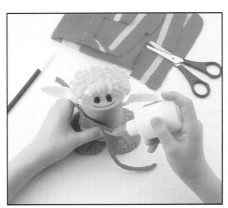

5 Cut a little apron out of the dish towel piece and glue it in place on the front of the body. Use construction paper if you don't have a spare towel.

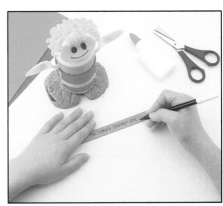

6 Cut a banner out of construction paper. Use your best handwriting to print The World's Greatest Cook! Glue it to the front of the trophy.

The World's Greatest . . .

It's fun to invent other "World's Greatest" trophies. What could you use to make a trophy for a fisherman, a computer whiz, a football player, or your favorite babysitter?

. . . Artist. An empty paint bottle and a spray can lid make the body for this talented artist trophy. Add crayon feet, paintbrush arms, yarn hair and a cute little hat cut out of felt.

. . . Cook. Who's the best cook in your family?

. . . Golfer. Do you know someone who likes to play golf? Ask if you can have an old golf club cover, some tees and ball markers, and a little score pencil. Then surprise him with his own Greatest Golfer trophy!

World's Greatest Teacher

WORLD'S GREATEST GOLFER

. . . Teacher. Give this to your teacher on the last day of school! Use a chalkboard eraser for the body, with pink eraser feet, yellow pencil arms, thumbtack eyes, and hair made from the spiral wire from an old notebook.

Handmade Paper

The paper we use every day is made in factories. But handmade paper is much more interesting and great fun to make in your own kitchen. **Get permission** to do this project, or get an adult to help you.

You will start by making *pulp*, a goopy mixture of paper fibers and water. Tear scraps of paper into tiny pieces and blend them with lots of water. You can even let the torn paper scraps soak in water overnight to make it easier on your blender. To make a really strong piece of paper, grind the pulp in the blender for 2 or 3 minutes until only the fibers are left.

Materials needed:

Sponge

Scraps of paper and cloths or towels

Blender and water

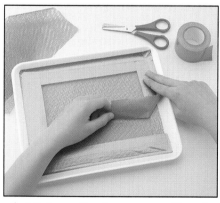

1 Make a dipping screen: Cut the center out of a clean foam meat tray. Cut a piece of window screen to fit the hole and tape it to the tray.

2 Tear stationery, computer paper, business cards, index cards, and envelopes into small pieces. Don't use newspaper, paper towels, or tissues.

3 Fill the blender ¾ full of water. Turn it on low and *slowly* add a handful of paper pieces. Use *lots* of water and not much paper, or you'll ruin the blender.

Plastic dishpan and a board

Piece of window screen
Foam meat tray

Scissors

Duct tape

4 Grind the paper into a soupy mash (called pulp). Pour the water and pulp into the dishpan half full of water. The pulp will float! Do this 5 to 6 times.

5 Slip your dipping screen into the water under the floating pulp. Lift it straight up, catching a thin layer of pulp on the screen.

6 Gently flip the screen over onto a damp towel. Pat the back of the screen with a wet sponge to release the layer of pulp.

139

Try adding things as you make pulp in the blender: dried leaves, grass clippings, flower petals, coffee grounds, *tiny* bits of cloth or thread, even spices to make scented paper. *Ask an adult* what is safe to put in the blender.

7 Lift off the screen and fold the towel over on top of the pulp. Repeat this process until you have several layers of pulp between layers of towel or cloth.

8 Place the stack of towels and paper on the basement floor or outside on the sidewalk. Put the board on top and stand on it to squeeze out the water.

9 Peel back the towel and *very gently* work your fingers under the paper and lift it off. Do this for each piece of paper, and put them on a flat surface to dry overnight.

140

You can also decorate handmade paper after you flip it off the screen onto the towel. Pat any small, flat object into it. Try dried flowers, strips of ribbon, or tiny stars and sequins. Then press the paper and let it dry.

Hardware Art

These rugged sculptures look especially good outdoors in a garden or patio. Rain and sun add a special beauty as the years go by. Start with plain, soft wood like redwood or cedar, an interesting piece of weathered wood from an old fence or barn, or a pretty piece of flat driftwood.

Collect interesting old nails and metal tools: nails, screws, bolts, nuts, washers, horseshoe nails, furniture tacks, hinges, drawer pulls, bottle caps, wire, and springs. Ask a carpenter for old bits of hardware, look for small machine parts, or get permission to take an old clock apart for its gears and metal parts.

Be careful. *Work slowly* to avoid accidents, and *ask for help* if you need it.

Materials needed:

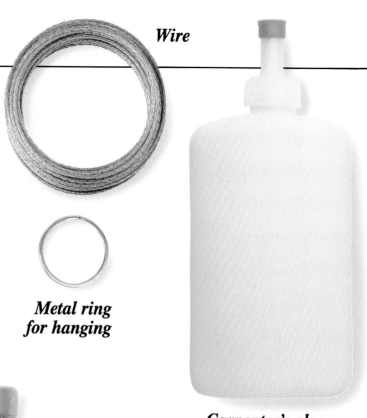

Wire

Metal ring for hanging

Carpenter's glue

A piece of wood and hammer

Metal pieces, pencil and paper

1 Design your picture on paper before you begin. Try drawing an animal — birds and fish are good — or a face or a giant sunflower.

2 Sketch your design onto the wood. Hammer rows of nails or tacks into the wood, following your outline. Fill in the shapes with other pieces of hardware.

3 Pound the hardware firmly into the board. Wire things onto staples to hold them in place, or use carpenter's glue to stick things in place.

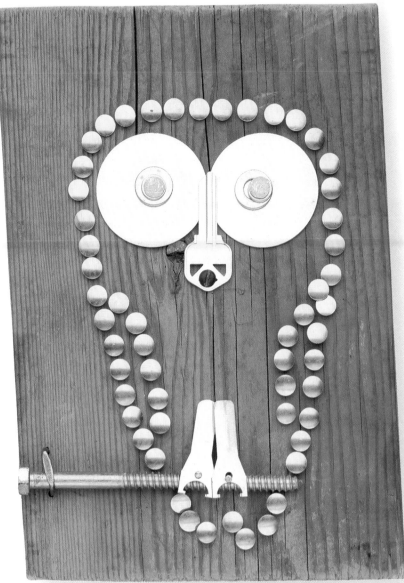

Abstract designs are fun to make. You can work from a sketch or just start hammering nails into the wood, making interesting patterns, and adding bits of hardware wherever you like. Attach a metal ring to the back or top of your finished sculpture so it can be hung like a picture.

Hardware Owl

Special Scents

Make fragrant bundles for Mom, Dad, Grandma, even your pet dog or cat! Follow these recipes or create your own—let your nose be your guide. Whenever you use something that needs to be dried, like lemon or orange peel or flower petals, spread them out on a plate and set them in a warm, dark place for one week. Ideas for scented gifts you can make are on the next two pages.

Spicy mix

Peel an orange and cut the peels into small squares and dry them. Put a cinnamon stick into a sock and pound it into small chunks with a hammer. Mix equal parts of dried orange peel, cinnamon chunks and whole cloves.

Aromatic mix

Gather needles from a pine tree and dry them. Mix a handful of dry pine needles with several spoonfuls of dried herbs such as rosemary, oregano, bay leaves and thyme.

Flower mix

Gather flower petals, especially rose petals, and dry them. Dried petals smell great all by themselves, or you can sprinkle a few drops of perfume on them for even more fragrance.

Pet mix
Combine cedar chips (sold at pet supply stores) with drops of eucalyptus oil (sold at a pharmacy) for a nonchemical flea and bug repellant.

Mint mix
Gather fresh mint leaves and dry them, or use mint tea. Peel a lemon and cut the peels into small squares and dry them. Mix equal parts of dried lemon peel and mint.

Other smells
Combine any of these to create your own mixtures: scrapings from scented soaps and candles, dried lavender leaves and blossoms, herb teas, baby powder and bath crystals.

Scented Gifts

Sweet Hearts

Cut two heart shapes out of felt, each about as big as the palm of your hand. Spread a thin line of glue along the edge of one heart. Place a small amount of scented mix in the center of the heart and lay the second heart on top. Pinch the edges with your fingers until they stick together. Decorate the hearts with glued-on sequins, beads, glitter, lace and bows.

Sachet Bundles

Cut a 6″-square (15cm) or round piece of thin fabric (an old nylon stocking is perfect). Place a large spoonful of scented mix in the middle and pull the edges of the cloth up around it. Tie it with a ribbon or piece of yarn, and trim the top of the cloth to make a fluff above the tie.

Itty Bitty Bags

Cut a 4″ by 6″ (10 cm by 15 cm) piece of cloth. Have an adult help you stitch up three sides of the bag, inside out. Then turn it right side out, fill it with scented mix, and tie it closed with a piece of string or yarn. If you stuff them with pet mix, itty bitty bags become natural "mothballs."

Pet Pillow

Have an adult help you sew a cushion (like a bag but bigger, and easier to sew on a sewing machine). Make it big enough for your pet to sleep on, and stuff it with pet mix. Or have an adult help you stitch up a bandana and stuff it with pet mix for a natural flea collar.

Gifts for Men, Women and Babies

Make a small cushion for dad or grandpa by stuffing one of their old ties. Mom or grandma might like a little basket filled with scented mix. Make a bundle for a baby by stuffing a bootie with scented mix. Tie it closed with a pink or blue ribbon.

Seashell Boats

Fill little shells with scented mix. Wrap the whole shell with a piece of nylon stocking, lace or netting. Tie it with a ribbon and add tiny shell decorations.

147

Gift Calendars

What's your favorite holiday? Is it Valentine's Day or Christmas, the last day of school or your own birthday? You can celebrate them all, and even invent new holidays as you make this special calendar. It's a great gift for someone to use and enjoy all year.

Materials needed:

Glue or clear adhesive tape

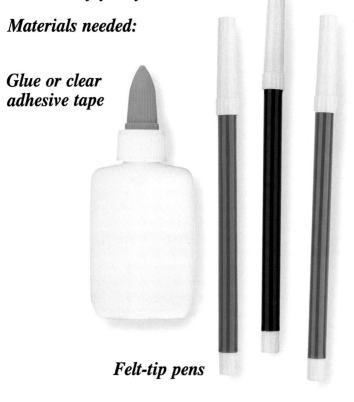

Felt-tip pens

Pencil

1 Trace or draw the boxes for each day, one page for each month, using a printed calendar as a guide (many businesses give them away for free).

2 Write the names of the days of the week across the top of each month and number the boxes. Write neatly and follow the guide calendar carefully.

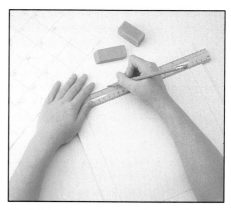

3 Make an art page for each month. Draw a frame around each art page about 1″ (3 cm) in from the sides.

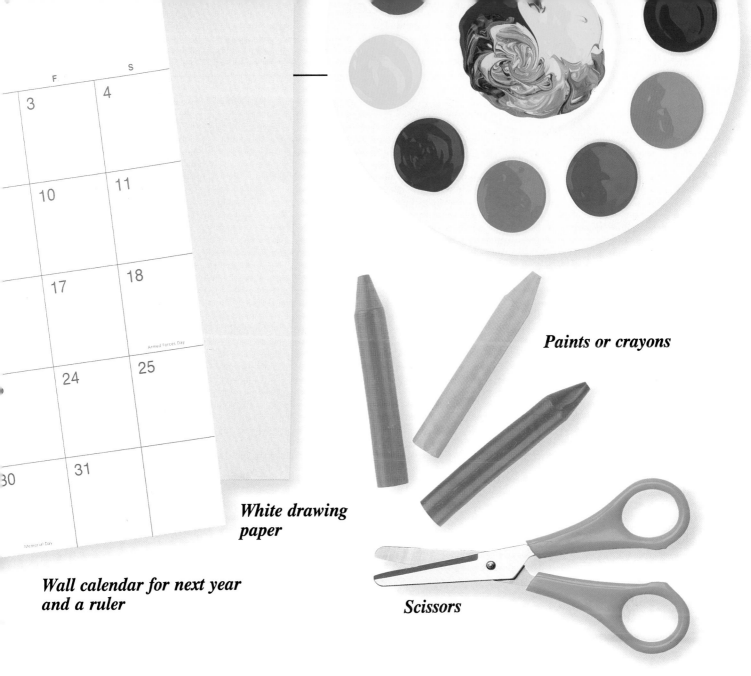

Paints or crayons

White drawing paper

Wall calendar for next year and a ruler

Scissors

4 Pick a holiday or special event and draw a picture for it—or draw a scene that celebrates the whole month.

5 Color each picture with bright crayons or paints. Draw small pictures or designs in the border and color them in, too.

6 Use a felt-tip pen to carefully go over all the words on your calendar. Use fancy lettering for a special look.

Art Pages for Calendars

Glue your pages onto the pages of a ready-made calendar. Or, tie, glue, or tape your pages to each other, using the ready-made calendar as a guide.

Container Mania

These bright and beautiful containers make great gifts because they have so many uses. They can be pen and pencil holders, flower-pots, kitchen utensil holders — make lots of containers to hold anything you need to store. You can decorate a container and then fill it with little things for a really special present. Start with a glass or plastic bottle or jar or empty can with a smooth edge on top, and make sure it's clean and dry.

Paper plate

Materials needed:

Container

White glue

Masking tape

Scissors

2 or more rolls of crepe paper

Water and bowl for mixing

Paintbrush

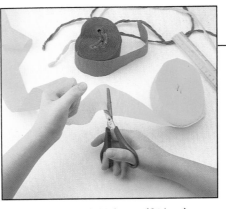

1 Cut several 8′-long (2½ m) strips of crepe paper. Twist them as tight as you can until they look like a rope.

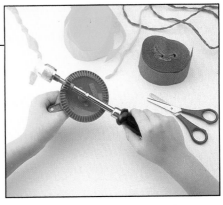

2 You can use a hand drill or egg beater to help twist. Tape one end of the crepe paper to the drill bit or beater and have someone hold the other end while you crank.

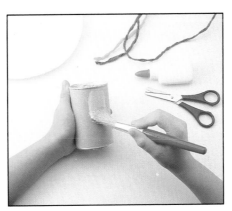

3 Squirt some glue onto the paper plate and use the paintbrush to smear a 1″ (3 cm) strip of glue up the side of the container.

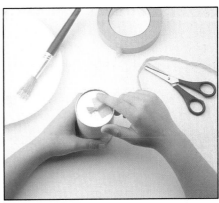

4 Tape one end of the crepe paper rope to the bottom of the container. Wrap the rope around the container, pressing it into the layer of glue.

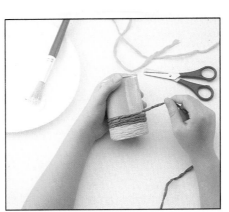

5 Push the rows of rope close together. Spread more glue if you need it. When you use up one piece of rope, cut the end, stick it into the glue, and start another.

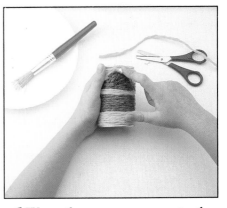

6 Wrap the paper rope up to the top and cut it and glue it down. If you want to use a cover on your container, leave a little space at the top so it will fit.

Crafty Containers

▼ Let the paper rope dry for an hour. Then mix equal parts of glue and water and brush the mixture over the top of the paper to protect it.

 ▶ Tear off little strips of masking tape and cover a bottle by overlapping the pieces. Go over it with black or brown shoe polish for a leathery look.

▼ Wrap a can with a cloth or plastic measuring tape to make a sewing kit. Glue a tomato pincushion onto the plastic lid and add a few stick pins. Fill it with a pack of needles and several spools of thread for a handy gift anyone can use.

▲ Twist colorful or shiny gift wrap ribbon with the crepe paper, or add fuzzy mohair yarn or bumpy chenille yarn for a different look.

▼ Glue crayons in a row around a small can to make a colorful pencil holder. Or glue a crazy collection of stuff to make a special "junk" container of your own design.

◄ Wrap a container with rope and add a bob or lure or some other finishing touch. Fill it with things your favorite fisherman will need on his next outing.

String Pictures

Geometry is the secret behind these elegant wall hangings. They look so professional, no one will believe you made them yourself! Start with fiberboard, cork, or foam-core board and cover it with felt or colored paper. Hang your finished string art by attaching a pop-top from a soda can to the back with a thumbtack.

Materials needed:

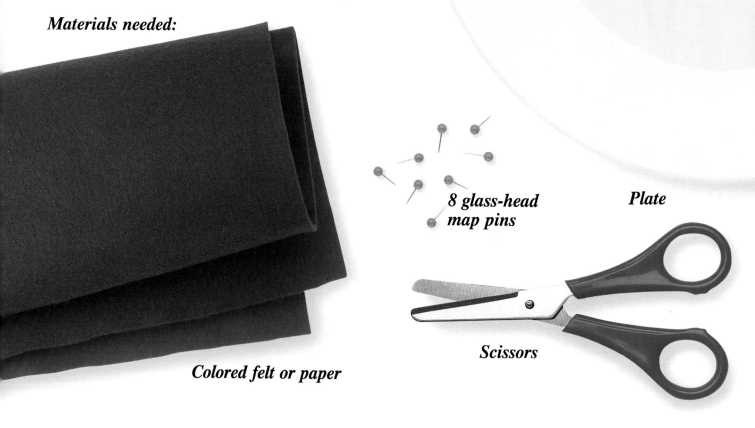

8 glass-head map pins

Plate

Scissors

Colored felt or paper

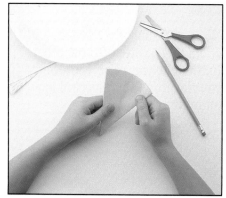

1 Trace a dinner plate on a piece of paper and cut out the circle. Fold it in half, then in half again (into fourths), then again (into pie-slice shaped eighths).

2 Unfold the circle and place it in the center of your covered board with one fold going straight up and down. Imagine the folds are numbered 1 through 8, with 1 at the top.

3 Stick a pin into the board at the end of every fold, right next to the paper circle. Leave the pins sticking up a little. When all 8 pins are in place, remove the paper.

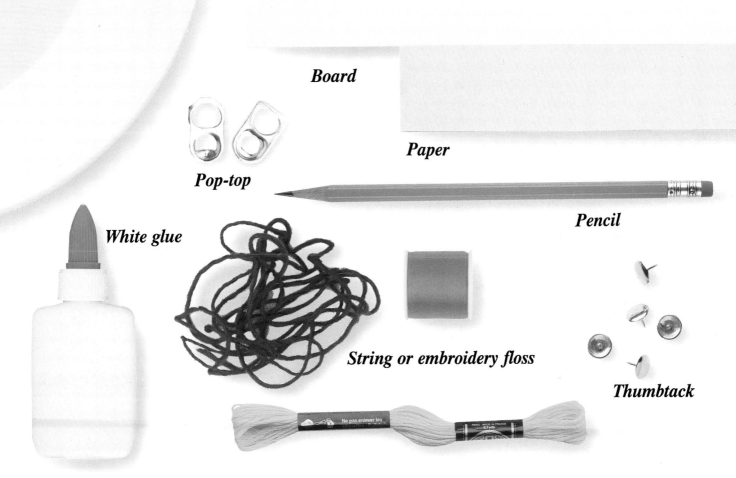

Board

Paper

Pop-top

Pencil

White glue

String or embroidery floss

Thumbtack

4 Tie one end of the string onto pin number 1 and begin winding around the circle. Go from 1 to 2, 2 to 3, and so on, making a loop (but not a knot) around each pin.

5 Keep the string tight (but don't pull the pins loose). After you've looped around the circle, go around it again in this order: 1 3 5 7 1 2 4 6 8.

6 Now go around the circle one last time, looping the pins in this order: 2 5 8 3 6 1 4 7 2. Make a knot when you get back to 2 and cut the string.

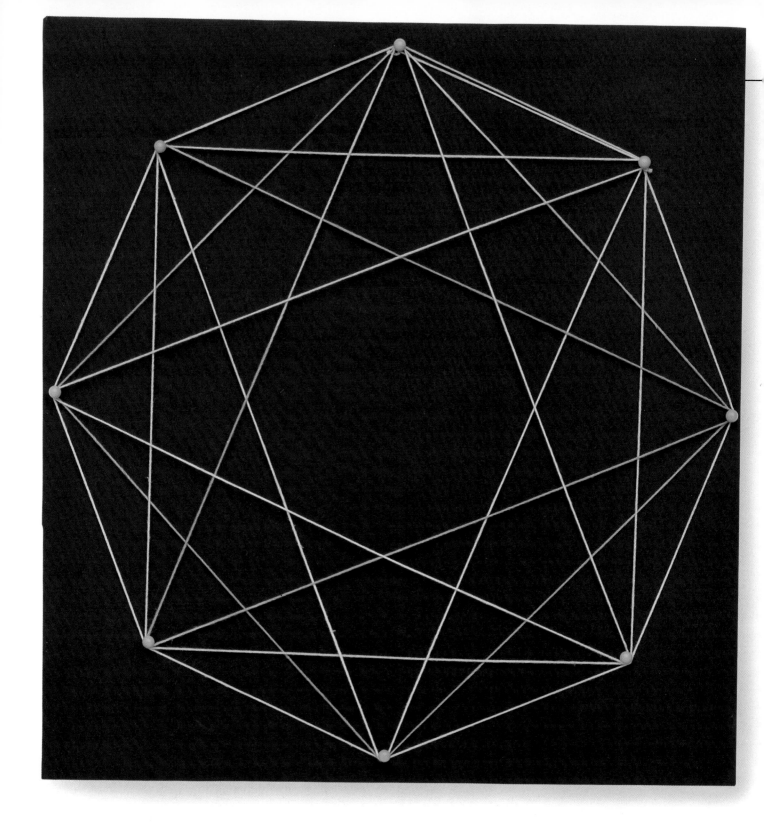

Try making a design using sewing thread—it's very delicate! Multicolored string and metallic thread look great, too.

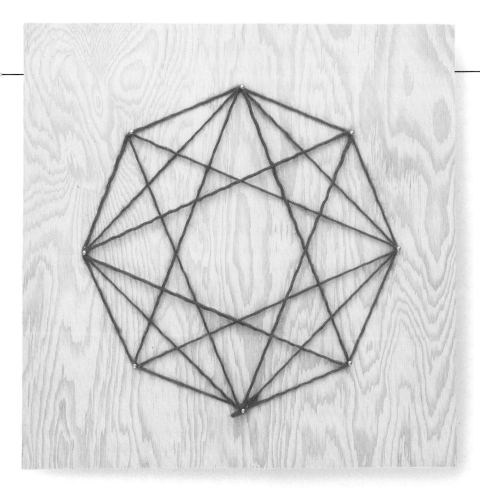

Try using different kinds of string. Yarn and twine look best in big designs. They're heavy, so use nails instead of pins.

Once you've mastered an 8-point circle, try a 16-point circle design! Fold the paper circle in half four times into skinny, pie-slice shaped sixteenths. Then follow the same steps, looping string around every pin, then every other pin, then every third pin, then every fourth pin, and so on.

Name Sculptures

Turn anyone's name into a special present with clay or dough. Make your own salt clay (that you let air dry to harden) or baker's dough (that you bake in the oven). Or use different colors of ready-made dough you can buy at toy stores, and let it air dry to harden.

Materials needed:

Salt clay

Mix 1½ cups of white flour, 1½ cups salt, 1 tablespoon of oil and enough water to make a smooth, soft clay (about ½ cup). Store in plastic in the refrigerator. Salt clay will dry hard if you leave it out overnight.

Nameplate Wall Hanging

1 Design the nameplate on paper before you begin. Make a full-size drawing so you'll know how big to make the dough plaque.

2 Roll a lump of dough with the rolling pin until it's ¼" (⅔cm) thick. Cut off the edges to make a rectangle.

3 Roll dough in your hands to make long snakes. Make a frame and the letters you need and press them onto the nameplate.

Baker's dough

Mix 4 cups of white flour with 1 cup salt. Stir well, then add about 1½ cups of warm water. Knead until the dough is smooth. Have an adult help you bake the things you make with bakers dough in a 300°F oven until they're golden brown. **Don't try to eat** your bread creations—they're for decoration only.

Paintbrush, pencils, and paper

Acrylic paint

Varnish (optional)

Knife and spoon

Yarn, string or ribbon, and felt

Rolling pin (and waxed paper)

4 Add decorations made out of dough: flowers and leaves, sports equipment, a teddy bear, or simple balls or heart shapes.

5 Poke two holes in the top corners of the rectangle with the bottom of a pencil.

6 Dry or bake the nameplate according to the recipe. Tie yarn, string or ribbon through the holes.

You can knead food coloring into salt clay before sculpting your nameplate if you wish. Or you can paint the clay after it dries.

This desk plaque was made out of baker's dough brushed with egg yolk before baking to make it golden.

Desk Plaque

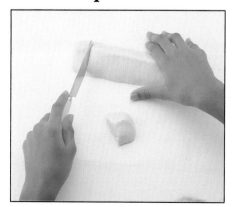

1 Roll a fat log of dough in your hands. Pinch and flatten it into a triangle shape. Trim the edges straight up and down.

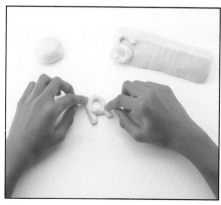

2 Roll snakes to form letters and press them onto one side of the triangle. Add decorations to the front and back sides.

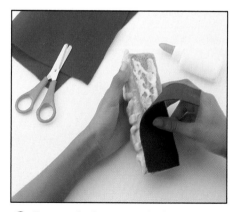

3 Dry or bake your desk plaque. Paint and varnish it if you wish. Glue a piece of soft cloth or felt on the bottom.

You can make other gifts with your clay or dough, such as ornaments, beads, and jewelry.

 You may want to have an adult help you brush a coat of clear varnish on your finished sculpture after it dries. It will protect it and make it shiny.

Free-Standing Sculptures

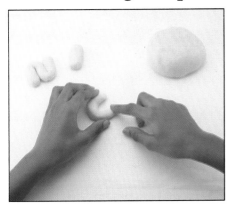

1 Roll fat sausage shapes of dough with your hands. Bend and mold them into big, puffy letters.

2 Gently press these fat letters together to make a name that stands by itself, either up and down or across.

3 Bake or dry your sculpture. Paint each letter a different color, with stripes and polka dots.

Pop Jewelry

Save the sticks from frozen pops or buy a bag of craft sticks at a hobby or art supply store. Use them to make pins, necklaces and key-chains decorated like all kinds of animals.

Materials needed:

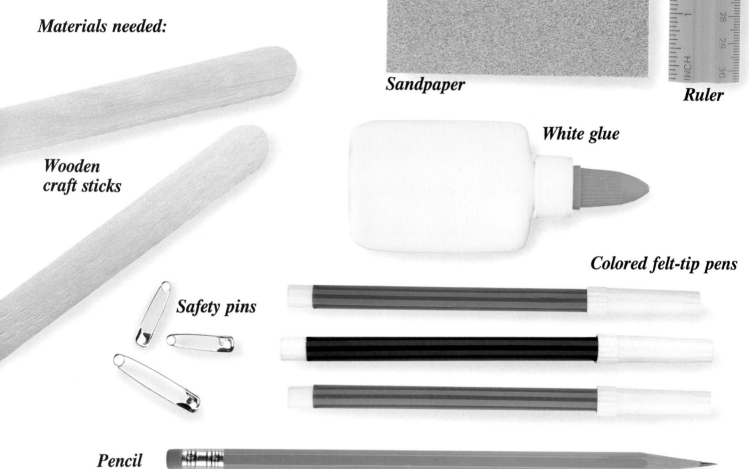

Sandpaper

Ruler

Wooden craft sticks

White glue

Colored felt-tip pens

Safety pins

Pencil

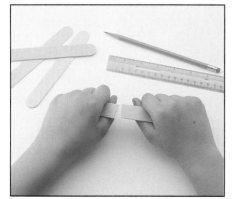

1 Draw a line across the stick 1½″ (4 cm) from the end. Scrape your fingernail along this line to make a groove. Bend and break the stick along the groove.

2 Rub the broken end with sandpaper until it's very smooth. Draw an animal design onto the wood with pencil, then color it in with bright felt-tip pens.

3 To make a pin, attach a safety pin to the back with a line of white glue. Hold the pin up out of the glue until it sets. Then let it dry overnight.

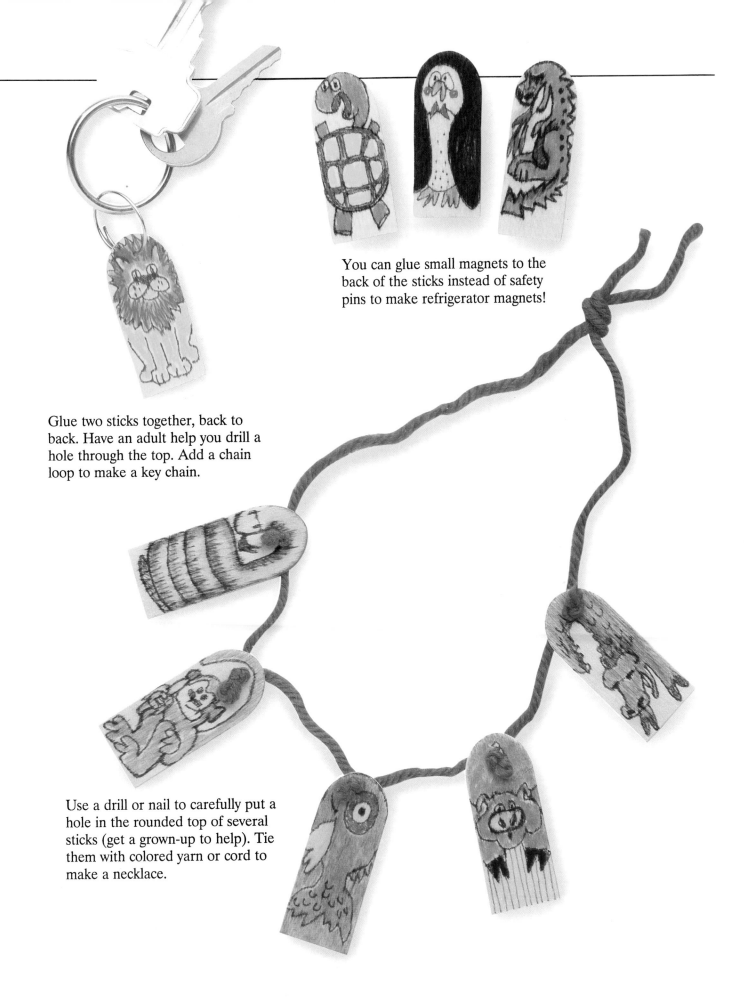

You can glue small magnets to the back of the sticks instead of safety pins to make refrigerator magnets!

Glue two sticks together, back to back. Have an adult help you drill a hole through the top. Add a chain loop to make a key chain.

Use a drill or nail to carefully put a hole in the rounded top of several sticks (get a grown-up to help). Tie them with colored yarn or cord to make a necklace.

Happy Wrapping

Get wrapped up in the fun of giving presents with wonderful gift wrap you make yourself. For a really special touch, make gift cards to match!

Materials needed:

Watercolors or tempera paint

White paper towels

Food coloring

Rainbow Wrap

1 For each color you want to use, mix 12 or more drops of food coloring with ¼ cup of water in muffin tins. Create your own colors!

2 Fold paper towels into squares and odd shapes. Dip the corners and edges into different colors— just enough to absorb some color without getting soaked.

3 Gently unfold the wet paper towel. Hang it on a clothesline or spread it flat on plastic or waxed paper to dry.

Muffin tin, a spoon, and water

Old toothbrush and a cardboard box

A variety of papers, ribbon, and yarn

Paintbrushes

Natural Beauties

Zebra Wrap. Paint 1″ (3 cm) black stripes across white paper. Use a photo of a zebra as a guide — the stripes get thick and then thin, and some stripes blend together.

Leopard Wrap. Paint a piece of paper light gold and let it dry. Then dip your fingers into a shallow dish of black paint. Make patterns of dots all over the paper with your fingers.

Moo Wrap. Big black patches on white paper look like the side of a Holstein cow. Tie this package with grass-green ribbon and add a tiny cow bell cut from an egg carton.

Wrap It Up

Moo Wrap

Crumple Wrap

Crumple Wrap

1 Crumple a sheet of newspaper into a ball and dip it into a shallow dish of paint.

2 Pat the newspaper all over a piece of construction paper. The wrinkled paper creates a beautiful crackle pattern.

3 When your newspaper gets too soggy, throw it away and crumple up a fresh piece.

Rainbow Wrap

Star Wrap

Star Wrap

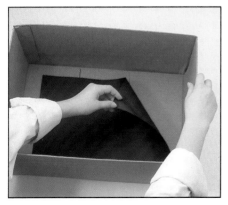

1 Lay a piece of dark construction paper in the bottom of a big cardboard box.

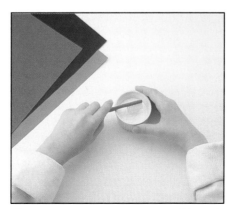

2 Dip the tip of an old toothbrush into white tempera paint. Hold the toothbrush in the box.

3 Rub your thumb across the bristles, splattering tiny dots of white paint onto the paper. Soon it will look like a starry sky.

Pop-Up Cards

Do you have paper, scissors and glue? Then you'll never need to buy another greeting card! Make your own birthday and holiday cards with these crazy pop-up critters. Put a special message inside the mouth for a great suprise. Look on pages 172-173 for other fun and easy cards to make.

Scissors

Materials needed:

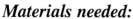

Crayons

Plastic eyes, feathers, string and decorations

Frog Card

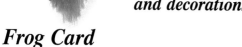

1 Fold two pieces of paper in half. One will be the card cover. Cut a slit across the other paper, from the middle of the fold to 2″ (6 cm) from the edges.

2 Fold the paper (on the bottom side of the cut) down to make a triangle. Fold it all the way out to the end of the cut.

3 Fold the paper (on the top side of the cut) up to make another triangle. This fold should be ½″ (1½ cm) in from the end of the cut.

*Construction paper
(9″ by 12″ or size A4)*

Felt-tip pens and a ruler

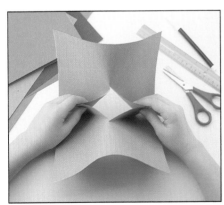

4 Open the paper flat and gently pull the triangle sections so they both fold toward you. Fold the paper in half again, this time with both triangles tucked to the inside.

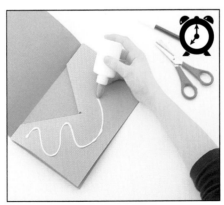

5 Spread glue on the parts of the paper that show. Wrap the cover around the outside. Press and wait a few minutes for the glue to set.

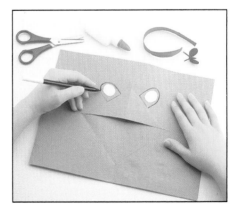

6 When you open your card, the triangle sections pull together to make a big mouth! Draw a face or use paper scraps or decorations to finish your card.

Make a green frog with a tongue that really dangles out the mouth. Add a fly for the frog to aim for!

Create a fierce fish with scissor teeth that just fit together as he opens and shuts his mouth.

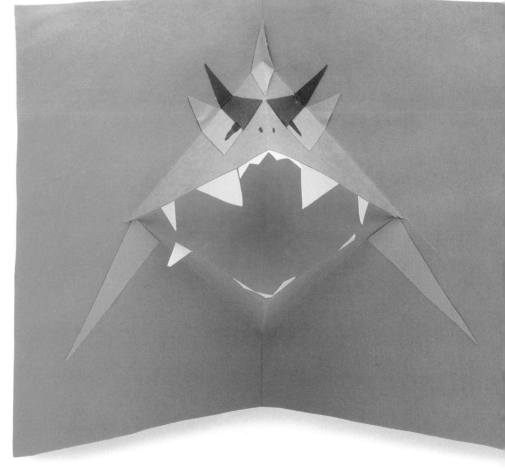

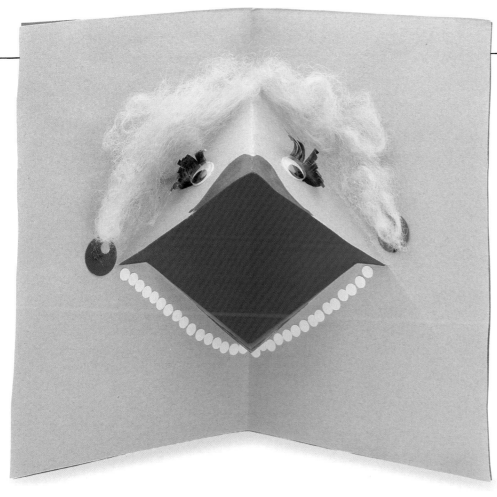

Make a person with wiggly eyes and string for hair. Or make a bird and use feathers to decorate.

Build a different kind of peek-a-boo card by drawing a house or castle with lots of windows and doors. Cut around them so they'll fold open and shut. Glue this picture onto another paper, being careful not to glue the windows down. Open them and draw faces or messages.

Other Greeting Cards

You're the Star
Make a photocopy of a photo of the person you want to make a card for. Cut out the face and glue it onto a folded paper. Draw and color a picture around it. Turn people into TV stars, sports heroes, clowns—anything!

Nature's Cards
Collect small leaves and flowers. Lay them gently between pieces of paper and set a heavy book on top for several days. When they're flat and dry, set them on the front of a folded card. Cover them with clear adhesive paper.

Part Five: Make Costumes!

A Note to Grown-Ups

Make Costumes! features twenty-five unique and diverse projects for making costume pieces. These costume ideas are so easy and so much fun, your kids will want to use the book to dress up for creative play throughout the year. Twenty-one complete costumes are showcased to fire the imaginations of girls and boys:

In *Make Costumes!*, kids learn how to make tops, knickers, capes, hats, accessories, hair, even shoes. The projects are open-ended, allowing for limitless creative expression as kids decide how to combine garments to create any costume they imagine.

Getting the Most Out of the Projects

These projects are fun for parents and kids to do together, and simple enough for kids to do on their own. Best of all, young "costume designers" will beam when someone admires a garment they've made themselves, something not possible with store-bought costumes or outfits adults make for them.

Costuming provides a wonderful opportunity for self-expression. Kids can dress up in a way that they don't normally. They can imitate legendary characters or create new ones. They can use costumes for make-believe, or for acting out favorite storybooks or movies or nursery rhymes. You might want to discuss with your child how to put on a staged play: how to write the story, make a simple set, and decide who will do and say what.

Collecting Supplies

The list of materials shown at the beginning of each activity indicates what was used to make the featured project. Suggested alternatives may require different supplies. Feel free to substitute! Almost anything can be turned into a costume. The projects are totally flexible to make it easy for you and your child to make as many costumes as you wish. Here are some household items you'll want to make sure you have on hand: scrap cloth or old sheets, pillowcases, tablecloths, curtains, towels, etc.; thin cardboard such as poster board and empty cereal boxes; white glue; masking tape; any old clothes, including pants, skirts, nylon stockings, and socks; paper bags—shopping bags, grocery bags, and lunch bags; aluminum foil; string and rope; plastic lids from milk or juice bottles; needle and thread; yarn; safety pins.

Almost any of the costumes in this book can be made out of paper instead of cloth, but costumes made out of paper may not last as long.

If you know how to sew, then you should sew cloth costume pieces together for strength and durability. If you don't want to sew, you can put costumes together with tape or glue, but your costumes may not last as long.

Tops

Tops are super simple to make. You can make beautiful long tops for costumes like witches, wizards, angels and movie stars. Or make a short top for a monster, pirate, ballerina or clown. The first step is always to fold the cloth in half so that your top will have a front and a back. Then you can hold it up against your body, with the fold under your chin, to see how long it will be. It's fun to cut shapes in the cloth or add sleeves. You can even make short tops out of paper shopping bags!

Trims

Decorations

Aluminum foil

Materials needed:

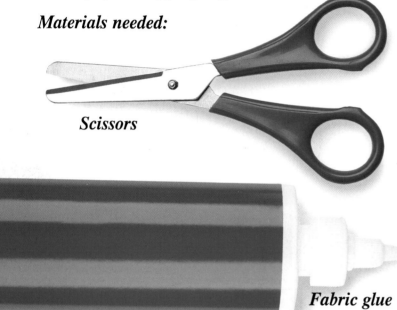

Scissors

Fabric glue

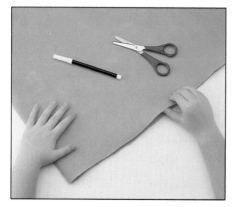

1 Fold the cloth in half. Hold it up against you to make sure it's the right length and wide enough to go from shoulder to shoulder.

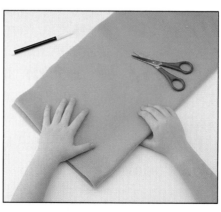

2 Lay the folded cloth flat. Fold it in half again so it will be long and skinny.

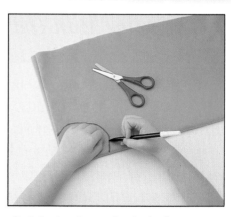

3 Mark where the hole for your neck will be. Make a fist and lay it on the corner of the folded cloth. Draw a line around your fist.

Paint

Yarn and needle

Paper shopping bags

Felt-tip pens

Paintbrush

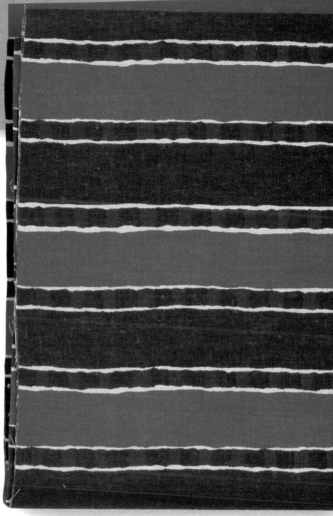

Cloth: sheet, tablecloth, felt

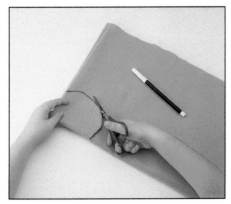

4 Cut the corner off. Cut it round (like the American Indian top on page 181) or square (like the Robin Hood top on page 180).

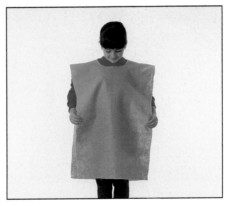

5 Unfold the top and try it on. You can trim it if it's too long. Cut the bottom straight across, cut a zigzag, or cut fringe into it!

6 You can sew up the sides, leaving holes at the top for your arms. Or just hold your top closed with a belt. Add fringe and trims!

Fun Tops

◄ Here's a clown top an adult helped sew, with sleeves and a fluffy collar made from scrap cloth. The "buttons" are milk bottle tops!

► The dragon top is a paper bag covered with cloth scales. You could paint the scales instead of making them cloth. The belly is felt with glitter paint stripes.

Sleeves

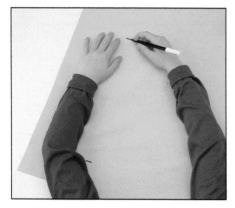

1 Here's how to add sleeves to your top. Cut two rectangles that are as long as your arm and as wide as from your elbow to your fingertips.

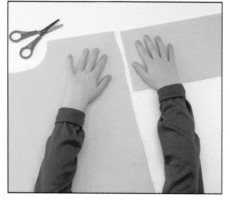

2 Fold each rectangle in half so they're long and skinny. Place them next to your top—put the folds next to each other.

3 Unfold the top and the rectangles. Sew or tape the pieces together.

◀ The monster's top is a paper bag painted to look like a jacket!

▶ This robot top is a paper bag with aluminum foil trim. The triangle is made of poster board. Can you see three bottle caps and fifteen noodles painted silver?

Paper Bag Top

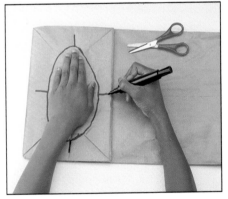

4 Fold the top and the sleeves in half again. Sew or glue the bottom of the sleeves. Sew or glue down the sides of the top if you wish (or hold it closed with a belt).

1 If you don't have cloth, use a paper grocery bag or shopping bag! Make an oval the size of your hand in the bottom of the bag. Draw four lines, as shown.

2 Cut out the oval and make small cuts where your lines are (for your head to go through). Now cut arm holes in the sides of the bag. Make them the size of your hand.

Topsy-Turvy

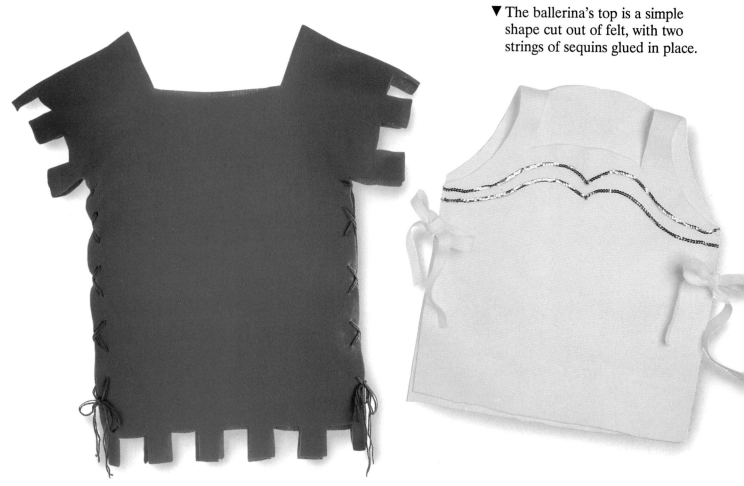

▼ The ballerina's top is a simple shape cut out of felt, with two strings of sequins glued in place.

▲ After you cut the neck hole for a Robin Hood top, unfold the cloth, cut up the sides and then out to make square sleeves.

Ballerina Top

1 Your top doesn't have to be square. You can cut it into a shape. Draw it on paper, cut it out, and try it on to make sure it will fit.

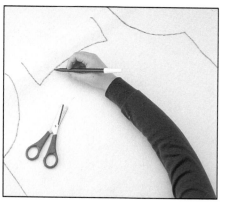

2 Make a short top following steps 1-6 on pages 176-177. Draw your shape lightly on the cloth. Then cut it out and decorate it.

3 Make four straps to pin or sew on the sides of your top, in front *and* back. Tie the back ones around your waist—*under* the front. Tie the front straps behind your back.

◀ A top with a ragged bottom is good for a pirate who's been at sea, fighting for treasure.

▼ This American Indian's top is long like a dress, sewn with yarn and trimmed with fringe.

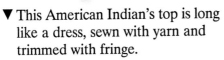

▲ The queen's gown is very long, with gold trim and beads and an old string of pearls.

Witch and Wizard

The best part of making costumes is putting the pieces together! Here are five finished costumes. You'll find more on other pages of this book. You don't have to copy these ideas! Use your imagination to design your own costumes.

The beard is made of fiberfill from a fabric store. It's painted gray and pinned to elastic.

Hat, page 212.

The elastic is attached to the inside of the hat, and goes under the chin from ear to ear.

Hat, page 212.

The witch's hair is fiberfill; it's taped to the inside of the hat!

His wand is made of a dowel rod painted purple and a cardboard star covered with glitter.

The wizard's wearing white gloves and holding an old glass ball flower holder.

Have an adult help you paint your face witchy green with warts!

Top, pages 176-177.

These fingernails are plastic containers florists use. They fill them with water and put cut flowers in them.

Pointy paper boots covered with silver glitter. See boots on page 203.

Boots, page 202.

Ghost, Robin Hood and Bee

An elastic strap holds his hat under his chin—it fits through holes cut in the sheet on either side of his head. See hats on page 212.

This ghost is a white sheet with a face cut out and red blood painted on.

He has Mylar tinsel for hair, glued onto the sheet.

The antennae are pipe cleaners and foam balls sprinkled with glitter and attached to a headband.

This bee's top is made from a pillowcase.

Aluminum foil chain.

Hat, page 213.

Weapons, page 216.

Wings, page 214.

Top, page 180.

The bee's stinger is like a cone-shaped hat (see pages 210-211). It's covered with fabric and painted. It has a gold pipe cleaner on the end. Staple black elastic to both sides of the inside of the cone. Then wear the elastic around your front.

Boots, page 202.

Skeleton feet painted on old, black socks!

Knickers

Knickers are short pants. They stop just below your knees. You can make them look three different ways at the bottom: straight across, jagged, or "gathered" like the baby doll bloomers on page 186. Knickers are worn by baseball players and football players, golfers, clowns, babies and baby dolls, princes, monsters, and pirates.

Masking tape

Materials needed:

Paint

Safety pins

Scissors

Decorations

Paintbrush

Baggy Knickers

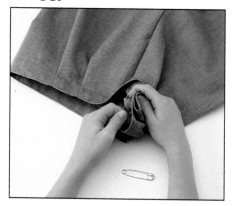

If the old pants you're using are too big, make "pleats" in the front. Pinch folds of material and pin them on the inside of the pants, like this.

Straight Knickers

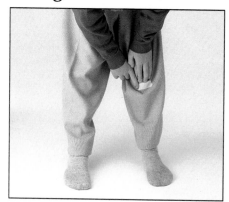

1 Put on the pants. Place your hand below your knee and measure to your fingertips. Mark the place with masking tape. Do this on both legs.

2 Take off the pants. Stuff the bottom of each pant leg up into the top of the pant legs until you get to the tape mark. Tape each leg all the way around the inside.

Old pants

Trims

Jagged Knickers

Measure how long your knickers should be (see step 1 on page 184). Take the pants off, cut the bottom of both pant legs off at the tape marks, and cut zigzags at the bottom.

Gathered Knickers

1 Measure how long your knickers should be (see step 1 on page 184). Cut the bottom of both pant legs off at the tape marks.

2 Measure one thumb-length up from the cut-off edge. Tape around the pant leg at that place and pull it tight to make a ruffle! Hide the tape with ribbon or lace.

Finished Knickers

◀ These clown pants are gathered knickers that an adult helped sew, with big polka dots cut out of felt and glued on with fabric glue.

▲ Soft colors and lace are good for baby doll bloomers.

◀ These prince knickers have fake fur for trim. Do you have an old, fuzzy rug you could cut up to make fake fur?

◄ For pirate knickers, cut fabric patches and sew them on with big stitches. Or paint them on!

▲ Ask an adult to help you use spray paint to add spooky black stripes to monster knickers.

▲ Here are knickers an athlete would wear—with knee patches!

187

Animal Heads

Animal heads are easy to make out of a towel and a matching washcloth. You can be any animal you want—just find a towel that's the right color.

Materials needed:

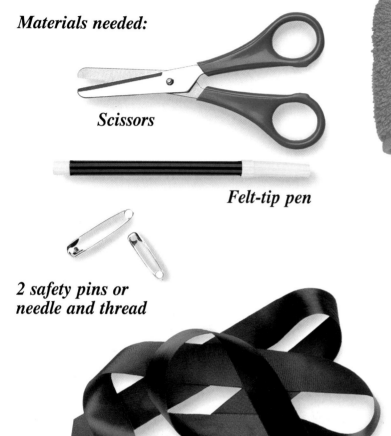

Scissors

Felt-tip pen

2 safety pins or needle and thread

Wide ribbon

Towel

Washcloth

1 Lay the towel flat. Fold one long side of the towel up. The folded part should be as wide as your hand.

2 Put the towel on, with the folded part in front. Tie the ribbon around your neck to hold it in place. Mark where the ears should be.

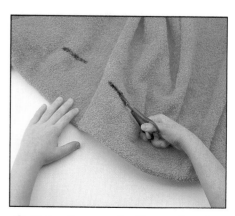

3 Take the towel off your head and make cuts where each ear mark is.

Dragon

A dragon has "spines" on his head instead of ears. Fold washcloths in half diagonally and sew or pin the folded edges to the towel. To make them stand up, glue pipe cleaners between the folded washcloth halves.

Tiger

Cut stripes out of black felt and glue them onto your tiger head. When you wear it, tuck the extra towel into the neck of your shirt.

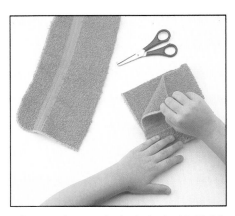

4 Cut the washcloth in half. Fold each cut piece in half.

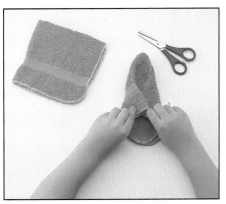

5 Put the fold on the left. Now fold one side to the left and one to the right to make a pointy ear shape. Do this for each ear.

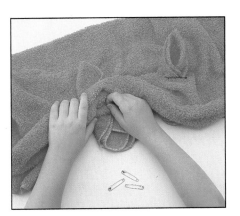

6 Fit the bottoms of the ear shapes into the cuts. Pin or sew the ears in place on the inside of the towel head.

Clown, Mermaid and Robot

Hat,
page 212.

Have an adult help
you design and paint
a clown face with
face paint.

Wrist bands made of
foil match the robot's
paper top.

Bow tie,
page 215.

The robot's
headpiece is a knit
cap with scouring
pads pinned on and
pipe cleaners stuck
in it!

Top,
page 178.

Knickers,
page 184.

Walkie-talkie,
page 215.

This mermaid's
gown is a big onion
sack from a food
market, with holes
cut for the head and
arms. She's wearing
it over a long slip
dyed green.

Hair,
page 197.

Top,
page 179.

Shoes,
pages 206-207.

Boots,
page 203.

Ballerina and Dragon

Have an adult help you design and paint a dragon face with face paint.

Head, pages 188-189.

Cut some washcloths in half diagonally, and tie them end to end to make a long tail. You can sew them or pin them to the towel hood.

The ballerina's headband is stiff paper covered with glittery stars. It's glued to elastic that was cut to fit her head.

Top, page 178.

Top, page 180.

Feet, page 205.

Get permission to wear a big, ruffly slip for a ballerina skirt.

Capes

It's fun and easy to make capes for great costumes like a king and queen, devil, vampire, witch or wizard, or superhero. You decide whether your cape should be long or short. You can make a cape out of almost anything: an old skirt, sheet, tablecloth, curtain, towel or shower curtain.

Materials needed:

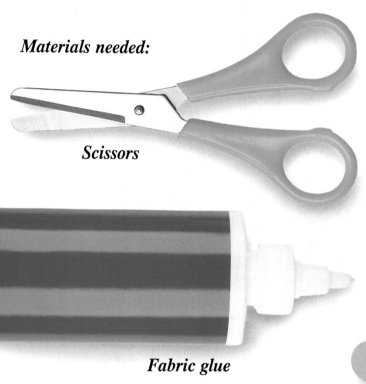

Scissors

Fabric glue

Shower curtain or other cloth

Ribbon and decorations

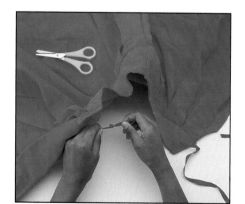

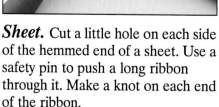

Skirt. Cut all the way up one side of a skirt. Make a hole on each side of the cut at the top. Put a piece of ribbon through each hole. Tie a knot in each ribbon on the inside of the cape.

Sheet. Cut a little hole on each side of the hemmed end of a sheet. Use a safety pin to push a long ribbon through it. Make a knot on each end of the ribbon.

Shower curtain. Get permission to use a cloth shower curtain. Put a ribbon through the holes at the top. Gather it around your shoulders and tie a knot on each end.

Queen Cape

Superhero Cape

If the skirt has a zipper, you can cut out all the stitches and then take out the zipper.

Wizard Cape

Add decorations to your cape: sequins, and planets, moons, and stars cut out of shiny fabric make this wizard's cape special.

Armor

Fruit trays, free from a grocery store or fruit market, can become a suit of armor for a knight, or a shell for a turtle. Just add paint and a few decorations!

2 fruit trays

Materials needed:

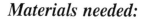

Decorations

Felt

Paint

Paintbrush

Ribbon

Turtle

1 Paint and decorate one fruit tray to look like the belly of a turtle and one to look like his back. It can look real or silly.

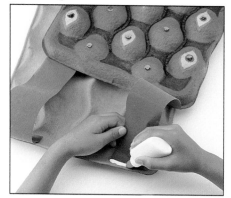

2 Make straps to go over your shoulders. Glue or tape them to the top on the inside of each painted fruit tray.

3 Make a belt to go all the way around your middle. Or poke holes in the sides of the fruit trays and tie a ribbon at each hole.

Turtle and Knight

A natural stick becomes a spear when you make a spearhead out of foil.

The knight's helmet is two stiff plastic bags folded and taped to make a cap. It's decorated with foil-covered coffee scoops, strips of foam, scouring pads, felt, and feathers.

Make a headband of felt with green sequins to match the shell.

The collar is like a big felt dough-nut—with a hole in the center for your head. The edges were cut into a zigzag shape.

Cut a shield out of another fruit tray and glue a stiff paper handle on the back.

This felt belt goes all the way around and ties in the back. It has shiny tinsel in the middle.

See how to make paper boot tops on page 203. These are covered with foil.

195

Hair

It's fun and easy to make hair for your costume out of yarn, nylon stockings or rope. These are just three ideas—what kind of hair will you need for *your* costume, and what will *you* make it out of?

Do you know the story of Rapunzel? She was kept in a castle tower. She let her hair grow so long that the prince could use it to climb up the tower. This Rapunzel's hair is a fat rope, pulled apart into long twists. It's glued to the inside of a cone-shaped hat (see Hats, pages 210-211).

Baby Doll Yarn Hair

American Indian Stocking Hair

Mermaid Rope Hair

Yarn Hair

1 Cut long strips of yarn—the more the better! Make them all the same length. Tie a shorter piece of yarn around the middle.

2 Glue the yarn onto a piece of poster board about 8″ (20 cm) long. Cut a 14″ (36 cm) piece of elastic and staple it to both ends.

3 On the top of the hair, put a thin line of glue across the middle to hold things in place. Add a bow. Cut some yarn short to make bangs.

Stocking Hair

1 Put the body part of the stockings on your head. Decide where you want the braids to start. Put rubber bands there.

2 Take the stockings off your head. Cut each leg into three long strips up to the rubber band.

3 Braid each leg by crossing the left strip over the middle, then the right strip over the middle. Tie the ends with ribbons.

Rope Hair

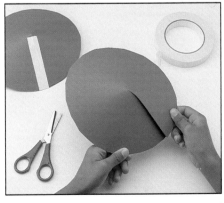

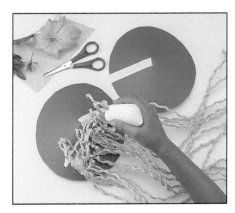

1 Cut two paper circles the size of the top of your head. Cut into the middle of each circle. Overlap the cut edges and tape them to make two cones.

2 Cut long pieces of rope. Pull apart the different sections to make long, curly strings.

3 Make a rope sandwich! Glue the curly rope onto the top of one of the paper cones. Then glue the other cone on top of the rope. Decorate the top cone to be a hat.

Angel and Devil

A paper headband is covered with sparkly trim from a fabric store. The halo is wire garland from a craft store.

The pitchfork is wire attched to a dowel rod from a hardware store. It's covered with felt and glitter.

The angel's top has two layers: a white sheet and a sheer curtain. The collar is scrap cloth folded to make a ruffle.

The devil's horns are wire attached to a headband. They're covered with felt and glitter.

Hair, page 197.

Top, pages 176-177.

Have an adult help you paint your face red and black for a real devilish look!

Wings, page 214.

The tail is a stretched-out wire coat hanger covered with felt and glitter.

Slippers, page 205.

Boots, pages 201 and 202.

Monster and Superhero

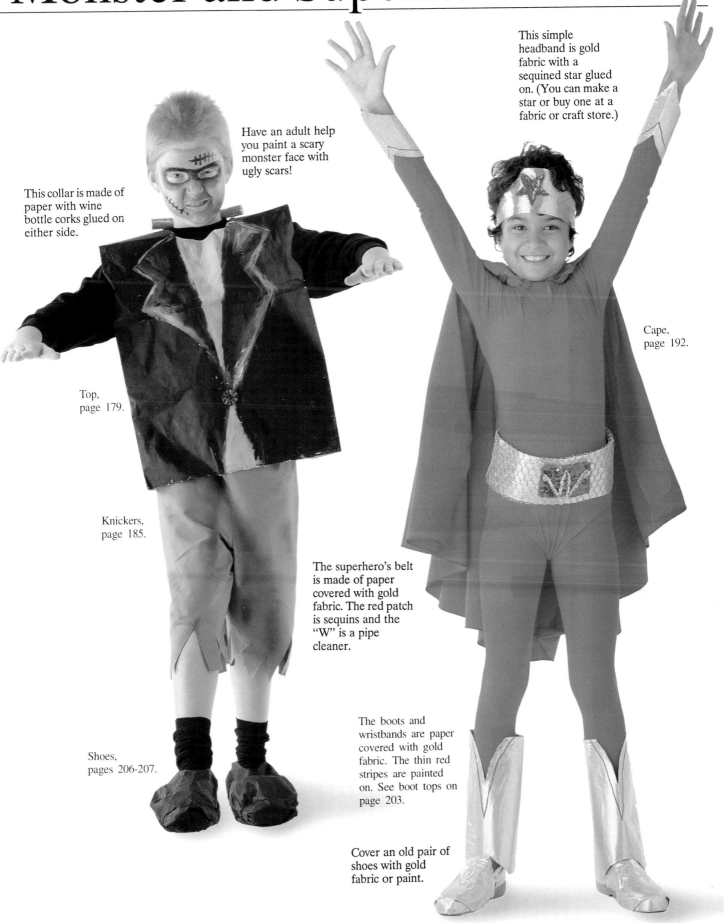

This simple headband is gold fabric with a sequined star glued on. (You can make a star or buy one at a fabric or craft store.)

Have an adult help you paint a scary monster face with ugly scars!

This collar is made of paper with wine bottle corks glued on either side.

Cape, page 192.

Top, page 179.

Knickers, page 185.

The superhero's belt is made of paper covered with gold fabric. The red patch is sequins and the "W" is a pipe cleaner.

The boots and wristbands are paper covered with gold fabric. The thin red stripes are painted on. See boot tops on page 203.

Shoes, pages 206-207.

Cover an old pair of shoes with gold fabric or paint.

Shoes

Special shoes are the finishing touch to almost any costume. It's easy to decorate old shoes or ballet slippers. Or, make big clown shoes or animal paws out of paper lunch bags. Make your own boots out of cloth or paper. Make felt moccasins. Old socks can become bird feet. Use your imagination, and you can make any kind of feet you need!

Paint

Needle and thread

Scissors

Materials needed:

Glue

Decorations

Stapler (or tape)

Markers

Paintbrush

Old socks

Cardboard (or heavy paper)

Lunch bags and grocery bags

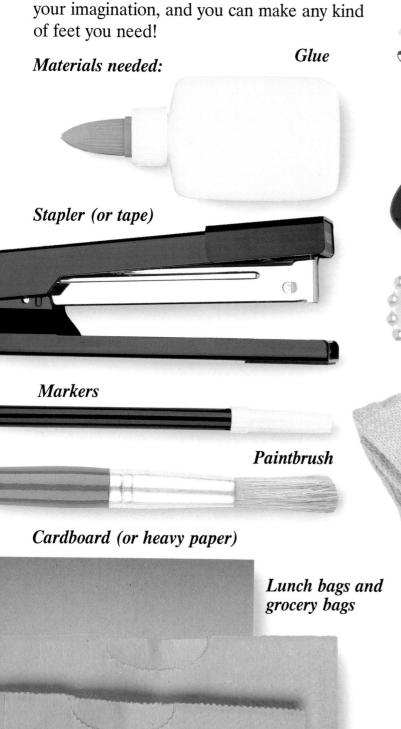

Devil Boots

Here's a sample of the kinds of shoes you can make and where to find directions: devil boots out of red felt and glitter (page 202), baby moccasins made with fabric and yarn (page 205), and angel shoes—ballet slippers with a cardboard piece on top (page 205).

Baby Booties

Angel Shoes

Beads and rice glued on top look like jewels!

Boots

Witch Boots

These cloth boot tops have pointy toes you can stuff with cotton or newspaper. Sew or tape elastic to go under your shoe.

Robin Hood Boots

Cloth Boot Tops

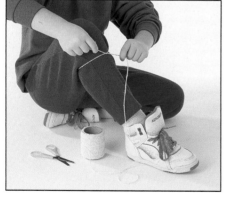

1 Wrap string around your leg where you want the top of the boot to be. Cut the piece of string that fits around your leg. Fold it in half and cut it at the fold.

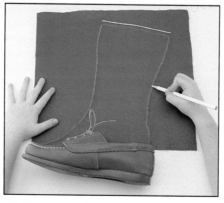

2 Lay one of your shoes sideways. Draw the side of a boot coming up from the shoe. Make the top of the boot as wide as the short pieces of string you cut.

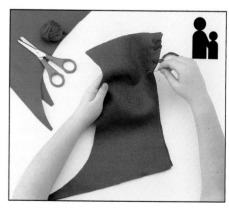

3 Cut four of the boot shapes out of cloth. Have an adult help you sew two together for each boot. Leave the bottom open so your shoe will stick out.

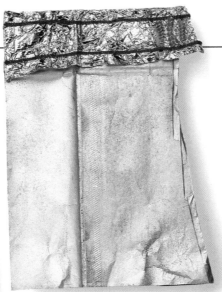

Robot Boots

Covering your shoes with aluminum foil will make them match your silver boot tops.

Pirate Boots

These boot tops are made of paper grocery bags covered with black felt. The buckles are cardboard covered with gold paper.

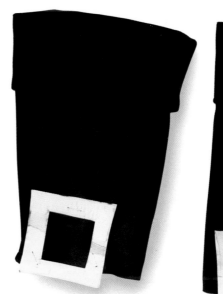

Paper Boot Tops

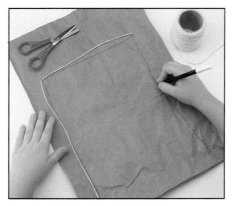

1 Measure a piece of string as in step 1 on page 202. Cut another piece of string that is as long as your leg from below your knee to the top of your foot.

2 Put these two pieces of string on a grocery bag in the shape of an upside-down L. Draw the side of a boot using the strings as a guide.

3 Cut four of these paper shapes. Tape two of them together for each boot. Paint them and decorate them. Wear them over the top of your shoes.

Moccasins, Slippers and Socks

Queen (or Movie Star) Slippers

Moccasins

Here are three kinds of sock feet, from left to right: bird feet, tobi socks (with two toes instead of three), and dragon feet (shown on page 191).

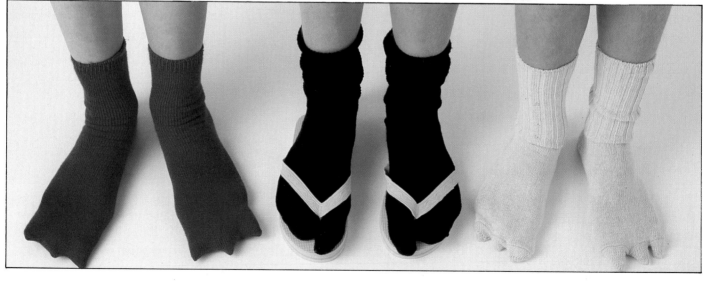

Moccasins

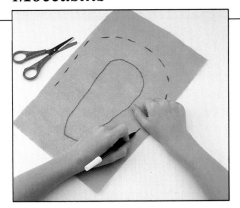

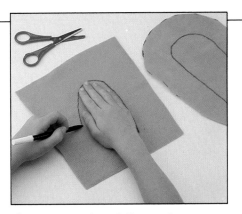

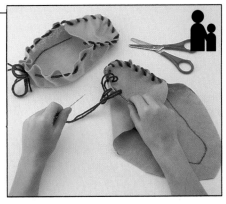

1 Stand on a piece of felt and trace around your foot. Then draw a bigger shape around your tracing using your thumb to measure. Cut out two of these.

2 Lay your hand flat and trace around it. Cut two of these shapes.

3 Have an adult help you sew the two pieces together with thick yarn. Decorate your finished moccasins with fabric trim or pompons.

Fancy Slippers

1 Lay your hand flat on a piece of cardboard. Draw an oval or triangle around your fingertips. Cut out two of these shapes.

2 Paint the cardboard shape, or cover it with felt the color of your ballet slipper. Add decorations. Make the two pieces match.

3 Roll a piece of masking tape. Stick the tape to the bottom of the cardboard piece and tape it to the top of your ballet slipper.

Sock Feet

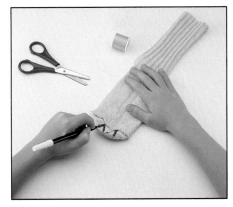

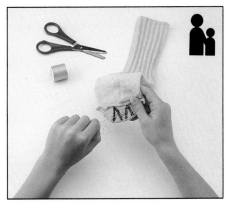

1 Get permission to use a pair of socks the color you want for the feet. Turn each sock inside out and draw two V's in the toe.

2 Have an adult help you stitch on the lines of the "V" shapes. Make lots of stitches.

3 Cut the middle of the V's. Turn the socks right-side-out and stuff newspaper scraps in the toes. Wear the sock feet over your shoes.

Big Shoes and Feet

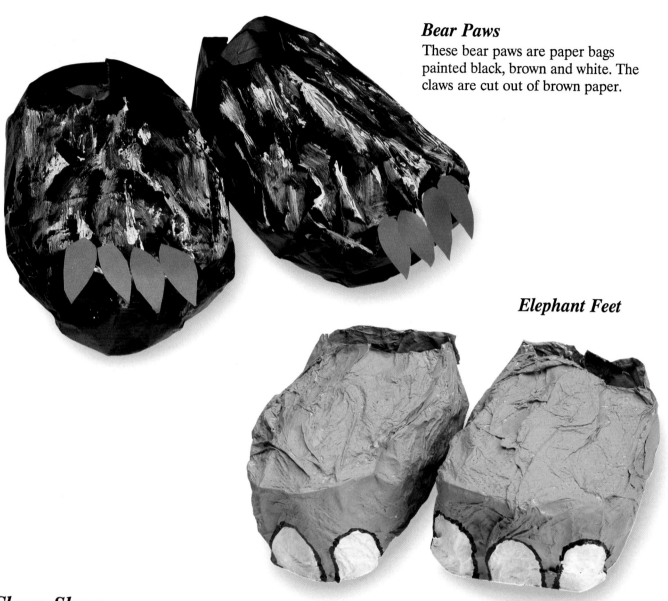

Bear Paws

These bear paws are paper bags painted black, brown and white. The claws are cut out of brown paper.

Elephant Feet

Clown Shoes

1 Make big paper shoes to wear over the top of your real shoes! For each shoe, put two lunch bags together, one inside the other.

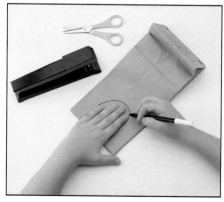

2 Put your fingers flat at one end. Draw an oval around your fingertips.

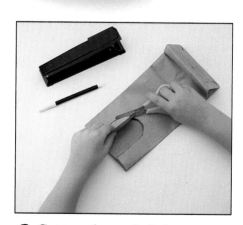

3 Cut out the oval. Only cut through the top two layers of bags (don't cut the bottom yet).

Monster Shoes

Finished Clown Shoes
Slide your foot, with a shoe on, into the clown shoe and tape the ends around the back of your foot.

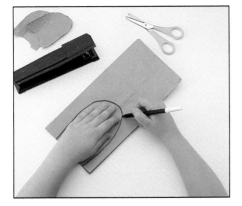

4 Turn the bags over. Lay your hand on the end of the bag that you just cut. Draw an oval around your whole hand and cut it out.

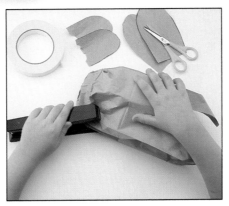

5 Pinch the toe end of the shoe into a round shape. Hold it with tape or staples.

6 Stuff the toes with newspaper. Paint and decorate. The big hole goes on the bottom and the small hole goes on the top.

Pirate and Bride

Sword,
page 216.

Wear a scarf or
bandana on your
head.

The eye patch is
black felt sewn onto
black elastic.

This bride's gown,
veil and sash are
made of old curtains!

The veil is attached
to a ribbon, tied like
a headband, with
fake pearl trim on
the front.

This necklace
is an old belt.

Top,
pages 176-177
and 181.

The sash was a ruffly
valance (the part of
curtain that goes
across the top of the
window).

A bouquet of silk
flowers and ribbons.

Knickers,
page 185.

The pirate's belt is
paper covered with
black fabric. An old
rag, folded in half
and sewn or tied
onto the belt, looks
like a pouch for the
pirate's treasures.

Boots,
page 203.

Slippers,
page 205.

Vampire, Indian and Queen

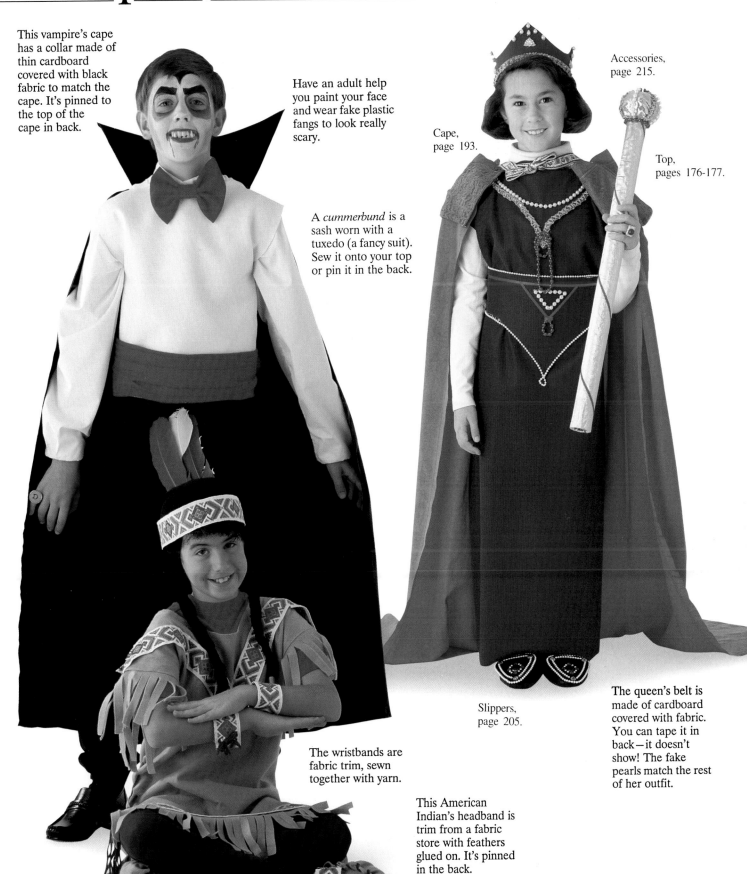

This vampire's cape has a collar made of thin cardboard covered with black fabric to match the cape. It's pinned to the top of the cape in back.

Have an adult help you paint your face and wear fake plastic fangs to look really scary.

A *cummerbund* is a sash worn with a tuxedo (a fancy suit). Sew it onto your top or pin it in the back.

Accessories, page 215.

Cape, page 193.

Top, pages 176-177.

The wristbands are fabric trim, sewn together with yarn.

This American Indian's headband is trim from a fabric store with feathers glued on. It's pinned in the back.

Slippers, page 205.

The queen's belt is made of cardboard covered with fabric. You can tape it in back—it doesn't show! The fake pearls match the rest of her outfit.

Hats

Hats are an important part of many great costumes. They're easy to make out of paper, paper bags or thin cardboard. You can paint them and add decorations and hair. Look through storybooks and encyclopedias for hat ideas, especially for characters like princesses, wizards, and Robin Hood. Then draw a picture of the hat you want to make, and use your sketch as a guide while you make the hat.

Masking tape

Clothespins or paper clips

Materials needed:

Glue

Felt-tip pens

Colored pencils

Paintbrush

String

Cone-shaped Hat

1 Measure your head where you want the hat to fit. Wrap a piece of string around your head. Pinch the string where the end touches it and cut it there.

2 Cut all the way up one side of a cereal box. Lay the box flat, with the printed side facing up. Cut off the flaps.

3 Roll the box into a cone shape until the big end is the size of the piece of string you cut in step 1. Hold the cone with clothespins while you measure.

Paint

Decorations and elastic

Scissors

Cereal box, heavy paper, large sheer curtain

Princess Hat

4 Cut off the bottom triangles so the hat has an even, round bottom. Wrap tape around the cone to hold it. Then remove the clips.

1 Place the hat on one corner of a big curtain. Tape the corner of the curtain to the hat. Roll the hat at an angle to the opposite corner of the curtain.

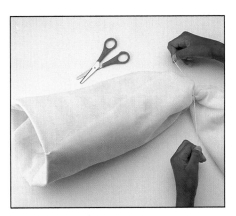

2 Push the extra curtain fabric up through the top of the hat. Tie it at the top with the piece of string you cut.

211

Hats

This clown hat is cone shaped (see pages 210-211). It's covered with fabric, with a feather stuck in the top. The yarn hair is glued to the inside.

The witch's hat is cone shaped (see pages 210-211) with a brim. It was painted black, allowed to dry, and then "painted" with glue to make it shiny and stiff.

The wizard's hat is cone shaped (see pages 210-211) without a brim. The stars and moons were "painted" on with glue and sprinkled with glitter.

This hat is a cap with a brim and a simple white ribbon decoration. Who would wear a hat like this?

Cap

1 Use string to measure your head as in step 1 on page 210. Cut a piece of heavy paper a little longer than the string and 3″ (7½ cm) wide.

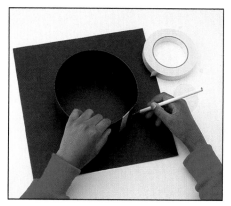

2 Tape the ends of the strip of paper together to make a ring. Set it down on another piece of paper and carefully trace around it.

3 Cut out the circle you traced in step 2. Tape it to the ring. Tape or staple a piece of elastic on the inside to go under your chin.

212

This blue hat is like the Robin Hood hat—two pieces of heavy paper taped together and painted. It's just a different shape. It could be worn by an army private or a flight attendant.

This Robin Hood hat was painted with green and blue-green paint, and decorated with a big button and feathers.

This princess hat (see pages 210-211) is decorated with gold trim from a fabric store. The extra roll on the bottom is made from a grocery bag, covered with fabric to match the hat.

This red hat is a cap without a brim. It's the kind of hat a hotel *bellhop* (the person who carries your suitcases to your room for you) would wear. Or, a dressed-up monkey!

Robin Hood Hat

Brim. Trace around the bottom of your hat. Cut out the circle. Measure one finger-length all around. Cut out this doughnut shape and tape it to the hat.

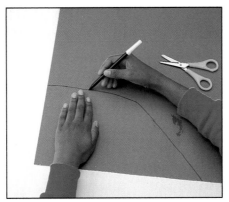

1 Draw a roller coaster shape on heavy paper. Make the highest part a little higher than the length of your hand. Cut out two of these shapes.

2 Tape the two pieces together all around the edges. Then paint your hat and decorate it. Tape elastic on the insides to go under your chin.

Accessories

Accessories are details that make a costume more special. Accessories are easy to make and *fun* — you can really let your imagination go wild!

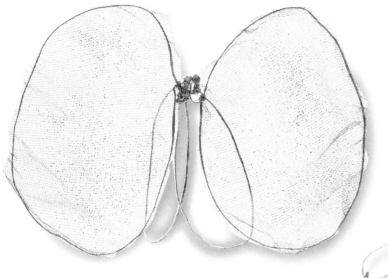

The bee's wings are made with gold wire from a craft store. Make two ovals for wings and two ovals to put your arms through. The wire is threaded through black netting that is sprinkled with glitter.

The pirate's earring is a gold curtain ring attached to elastic. The elastic goes around your whole ear! If you don't have a curtain ring, you can make one out of paper.

This angel's wings are covered with lots of white feathers. You can decorate yours however you wish!

Angel Wings

1 Put two wire coat hangers together like this and wrap masking tape around the middle to hold them.

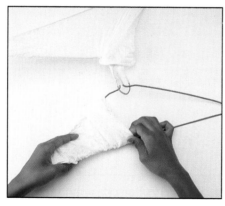

2 Cut the legs off of heavy nylon stockings. White is best for an angel. Cover each hanger with one stocking leg.

3 Tie the stocking legs together in the middle. Use a big safety pin to fasten the wings to the back of your costume.

The robot's walkie-talkie is a box wrapped with silver tape and covered with noodles that are painted silver. The antennae are black pipe cleaners.

A finished bow tie.

The queen's crown is a ring of heavy paper glued in the back. It's painted blue and has fake pearls and trim (from a craft store) glued on.

It's easy to glue paper, fabric, foil and beads onto old plastic rings to make rings for a queen, a vampire, or a bride.

The queen's scepter is a cardboard tube and a foam ball covered with gold fabric and ribbon and beads.

Bow Tie

1 Cut a piece of fabric 8″ by 12″ (20 cm by 30 cm). Lay it right-side-up. Fold each end in to the middle and tape it along the sides.

2 Turn the taped fabric right-side-out. Be gentle so you don't tear the tape.

3 Cut a thin strip of fabric. Wrap it tightly around the middle. Tape it in the back. Pin it to the neck of your costume.

Weapons

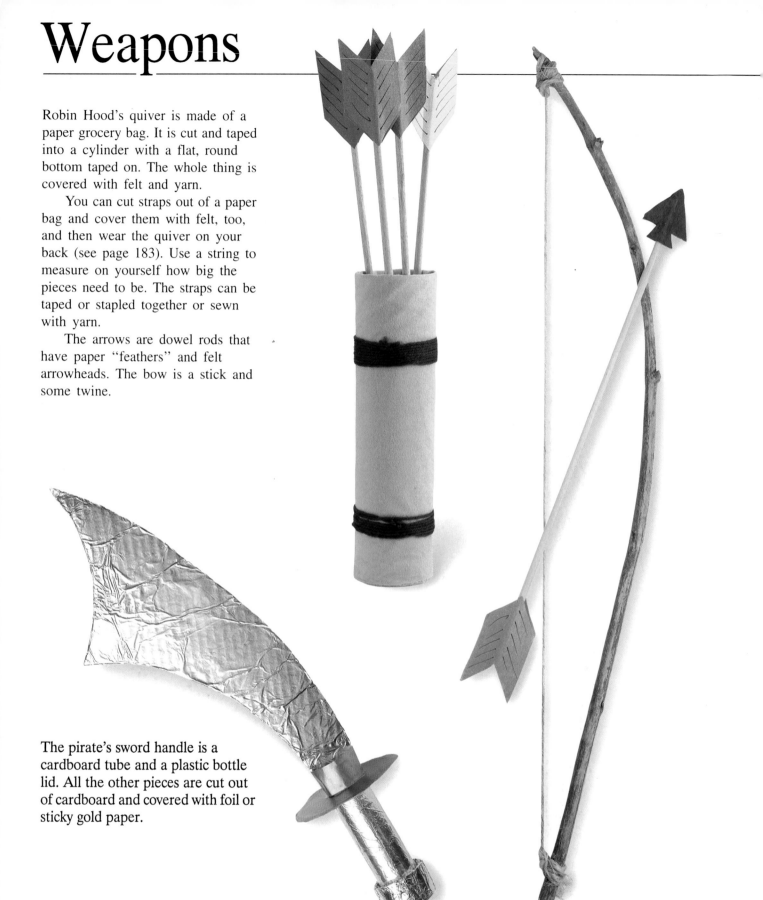

Robin Hood's quiver is made of a paper grocery bag. It is cut and taped into a cylinder with a flat, round bottom taped on. The whole thing is covered with felt and yarn.

You can cut straps out of a paper bag and cover them with felt, too, and then wear the quiver on your back (see page 183). Use a string to measure on yourself how big the pieces need to be. The straps can be taped or stapled together or sewn with yarn.

The arrows are dowel rods that have paper "feathers" and felt arrowheads. The bow is a stick and some twine.

The pirate's sword handle is a cardboard tube and a plastic bottle lid. All the other pieces are cut out of cardboard and covered with foil or sticky gold paper.